THE ULTIMATE HOME BOOK

Home Maintenance Tips to Save Money and Time

WHAT YOU WILL FIND IN THIS HOME MAINTENANCE GUIDE

You enjoy your home and want to maintain It in the best possible condition!

Keeping your home in good condition is important if you want to spend stress free quality time at home with your family. Although you may call a contractor for some issues, it is not always a necessity. A number of homeowners desire to perform some of the more basic home maintenance duties themselves.

If that is the case with you, The Ultimate Home Book is just what you need. In this guide, you will discover common sense methods of maintaining your home that will save you money. The information contained in this book is useful for homeowners who want to perform basic repair work themselves thus keeping home maintenance costs down.

Some of the topics covered in The Ultimate Home Book include:

- Plumbing Repair
- Heating & Air Conditioning Repair & Maintenance Tips
- Furnace Filter Replacement
- Roof Maintenance
- Tips on Making Your Home Eco-Friendly
- and Much More...

The best thing about this Book is that you can jump to any topic when you need it. Keep it handy as a reference guide for whenever a home maintenance or repair issue comes up.

The Ultimate Home Book. Deluxe Edition.
A Guide to Operating Your Home

Michael Casey of Home Inspection University and
P. Nathan Thornberry of The Inspector Services Group

Residential Warranty Services/The Inspector Services Group
698 Pro Med Lane
Carmel, IN 46032
www.InspectorServicesGroup.com

ISBN 978-0-692-35325-7

Design by Danelle Smart and Tiffani Blackburn
Edited by Jenifer Costner
Project Manager: Nathan Ehman

All other photographs courtesy of ShutterStock.com

Orders by U.S. trade bookstores and wholesalers. Please contact RWS
Tel: (800) 544-8156; Fax: (877) 307-7056 or Web: www.InspectorServicesGroup.com

Printed in the United States of America

CONTENTS

Plumbing | 12

Leaky Toilets | 13

Dripping Faucets | 15

Gutters | 18

Reduced Water Flow | 26

Showers | 29

Water Heaters | 31

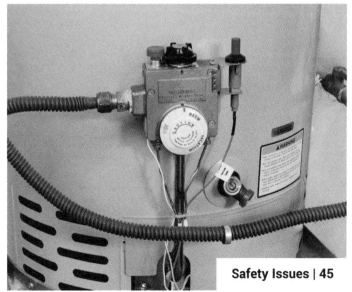

Safety Issues | 45

2 HVAC and Water Heater Maintenance & Repair

Refrigerators | 47

Dishwashers | 49

Microwaves | 53

Clothes Dryers | 54

Roof Maintenance | 62

Snow and Ice | 63

Caring for Your Lawn | 70

Decks, Fences, and Retaining Walls | 71

4 Roof Repair, Replacement, and Installation

   1. Keep the Attic Vents Open and Ventilating
   2. Seal the Attic Hatch
   3. Make Sure Vents Do Not Exhaust Through the Soffit
   4. Ensure Proper Insulation

   1. Inspect your Roof
   2. Check for Leaks or Water Damage in your Attic and at Ceiling Lights
   3. Inspect Roof Gutters and Vents
   4. Consider Installing a Roof Deck
   5. Inspect Ceilings and Interior Walls for Leaks and Staining
   6. Inspect Roof Decking and Fascia/Coping for Damage
   7. Clear Dust and Debris from the Roof

5: Exterior Accessory Care and Maintenance

Granite Tiles | 73

Exterior Maintenance | 81

Replacing Door Knobs | 87

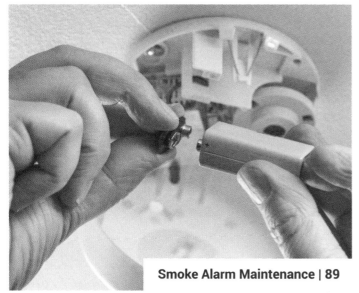
Smoke Alarm Maintenance | 89

6 Ceilings, Floors and Walls Maintenance

7 Building Exterior Maintenance

8 Door and Window Maintenance Tips

9 Home Safety and Security

10 Home Owner Resources

CHAPTER 1: PLUMBING MAINTENANCE AND REPAIR

A home provides invaluable comfort and protection for you and your family. Plumbing is the most important part of any home. Faulty plumbing can cause more than just high water use bills. It can also cause structural damage to your home and pose a major health risk to you, your children, and your home.

It is important to watch out for water leaks and unusual accumulation of water at the walls, floors, or ceilings. Here we will provide you plumbing maintenance and repair tips to avoid adverse effects of faulty plumbing. Any evidence of water leakage should be addressed quickly to avoid the consequential damages such as wood damage and mold growth.

Faulty plumbing can cause more than just high water use bills. It can also cause structural damage to your home and pose major health risks.

1.1. DIAGNOSING WATER LEAKS AT HOME

The EPA reports that in the U.S. water leaks due to faulty plumbing in a typical home cause the waste of more than 10,000 gallons (37,854 Liters) of water every year and ten percent of homes have leaks that waste 90 gallons (340 liters) of water a day.

Although the source of most of these water leaks can be located with a little effort, some can be hard to detect. In some cases, you must investigate to detect these water leaks. Here we will provide you 5 of the most effective ways to detect common water leaks in your home.

1. Unexpected Increase in Water Bill

The most obvious way to know about water leaks in your home is when there is a sudden increase in your water bills. It is important that you pay attention to your water bill, particularly the amount you typically pay each month. Any unexpected spike in your water bill may indicate that there is a leak in the plumbing. Be aware that most often people use more water during summers than in the winter due to irrigation of plants in parts of the country where there is a cold season(s).

2. Water Leaks at the Toilet

A leaking toilet is one of most common ways water is wasted in most homes. You should regularly check your toilet for signs of water leaks. If you see or hear the sound of water dripping a few minutes after flushing, it is indicative of a leaky toilet. At times you might hear the sound of the tank filling, this can also indicate trouble, when the toilet was unused. In the case of water leaks at the toilet that cannot be detected visually or audibly, you can place drops of food coloring in the toilet tank to make sure there are no leaks. Just place 4-5 drops of food coloring into the toilet tank and don't use the toilet for 15 minutes. If the bowl water remains colorless, there are no leaks. However, if the bowl water changes color, you've got a leak that is wasting water. Usually a new flapper will correct this type of leak.

3. Dripping Faucets

Another common cause of water leaks is slow dripping faucets at the sinks, showers, or tubs. The leaks may be small but it results in large amounts of wasted water over time due to the constant dripping. You should regularly check the faucets to ensure that there are no leaks. In case of any

A water meter that keeps on running is indicative of water leaks in the house.

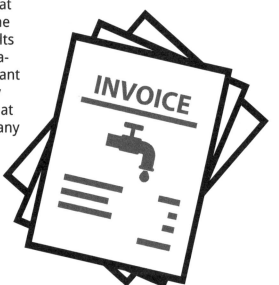

leaks, you should quickly have it repaired. One drip per second can add up to 3000 gallons (11,356 Liters) per year.

4. Check Your Water Meter

A water meter that keeps on running is also indicative of water leaks in the house. You should write down the reading of your water meter and check it again after a few hours without using water in the house. If the reading on the water meter changes during this time, it may indicate water leakage in the house and or the pipe from the meter to the house.

5. Wet Areas in your Yard

If you notice wet areas in your yard, there could be an underground leak. You should have a professional plumber look over the wet area. The plumber generally uses special tools and equipment to detect underground leaks without digging up the area to pinpoint the leak. Once located, the leak can usually be spot repaired. Many underground leaks are in irrigation systems, and may not leak unless the irrigation is operating so they would be intermittent.

1.2. REPAIRING LEAKY TOILETS

A leaky toilet is a common plumbing problem that you can probably fix yourself. You just have to know the right tools and equipment to perform the task successfully. Many times the leakage is simply repaired by installing a new flush flapper per the manufacturer instructions.

Here we will provide you information on how to fix a toilet leaking at the bowl to drain pipe connection (the flange) gasket, commonly called the wax seal. This type of leak usually shows up as water on the floor around the base of the bowl, or on the ceiling under the toilet. If not repaired quickly, this type of leak can result in structural damage and an unpleasant smell.

Materials You Will Need:
- A new wax ring
- Two 5/16-in. diameter water closet bolts (these usually come with the wax ring)
- A tube of silicone-based caulk, in a color to match the toilet
- A package of plastic toilet shims if your toilet is rocking

Step 1: Turn off the water at the shutoff valve below the tank or at the main water shutoff.

Step 2: Drain the tank and bowl completely and remove the bolt covers at both sides of the base of the toilet. A plastic cup and sponge can be useful for removing water in the tank and the bowl. Remove the water supply connection at the bottom of the tank. Have a rag handy to catch remaining tank water.

Step 3: Remove the bowl to floor nuts. Sometimes these are stuck and need to be cut with a hacksaw.

Step 4: Have someone help you and lift the toilet off the floor. Be prepared for some residual water in the bowl and tank.

Step 5: Lay it down on its side. An old towel us useful to protect the floor and the toilet.

A plastic cup and sponge can be useful for removing water in the tank and the bowl.

Step 6: Remove the old wax ring from the underside of the bowl and the flange at the floor. A putty knife works well for this task. Also, remove the old bolts at the floor flange. Inspect the flooring for any rot or damage, then repair or replace as necessary.

Step 7: Insert the new bolts and wax ring onto the flange at the floor.

Step 8: Have someone help you lift the toilet back onto and center over the flange at the floor on the new wax ring. The spud at the bottom of the bowl should insert into the center of the wax ring with the bolts protruding through the bolt openings in the bowl.

Step 9: Place your weight onto the bowl to set the bowl into the wax ring and get the toilet seated firmly on the floor. If your toilet is rocking, use plastic shims to obtain a level position for the toilet.

Step 10: Install and tighten the nuts on the bowl to floor bolts. Be careful to make snug but not too tight as it is possible to crack the toilet base.

Step 11: If necessary cut the bolts to allow for installation of the bolt covers. Install bolt covers. After reconnecting all mechanical connections, flush toilet and inspect for leakage. Caulk around base of the toilet to seal to the floor.

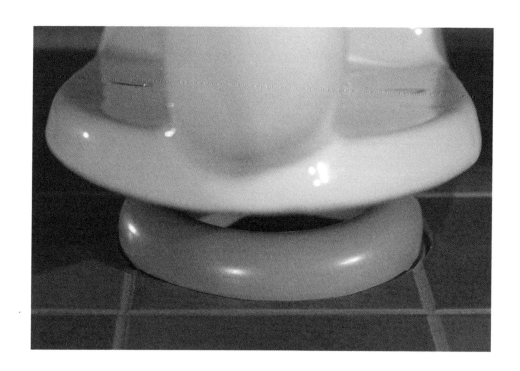

1.3. REPAIRING DRIPPING FAUCETS

Dripping faucets are another common annoying and wasteful plumbing problem faced by many households. The annoying drip not only causes irritation but also results in increased water bills. Fortunately, if you can identify the dripping faucets and obtain the necessary tools, you can fix the problem yourself. Here we will discuss how to repair dripping faucets yourself.

Things You Will Need:
- Pliers
- Adjustable wrench
- Appropriate washers or repair kit
- Sink plug or rag
- Phillips and slot screwdriver
- Occasionally hex key type wrenches

Step 1: Just underneath the sink you will find a handle that feeds water to the sink faucet(s). Turn the handle clockwise to shut off water to the faucet, both hot and cold. Open the faucet to confirm the water has been turned off successfully. If the valve at the wall has failed, shut off the water at the main water shutoff and test again. If neither stop the flow of water completely, it is time to call a plumber to repair/replace the valves.

Step 2: Plug the drain using the sink drain plug or a rag. This is a plumber's trick to prevent dropping small parts such as screws down the drain.

Step 3: Determine the type of faucet. There are four types of faucets which are installed in most homes. They include:

a. Compression Washer / Ceramic Cartridge Faucet,

b. Ball Faucet
c. Cartridge Faucet
d. Ceramic Disk Faucet

Compression washers and some ceramic cartridge faucets are easiest to identify as they have two screw handles, one for hot and one for cold. The other types of faucets have only one swiveling arm handle, which you can swing from hot to cold as desired.

Most of the time you have to take the faucets apart to know which type of faucets you have. Ball faucets contain a ball bearing with holes on rubber seats, cartridge faucets have rotating cartridges (usually plastic, some are brass), and ceramic-disk faucets have rotating ceramic cylinders. In some cases if you can see the brand name on the faucet you may be able to take a photo of it and obtain the repair parts from the local hardware store prior to dismantling.

The four most common types of residential faucets include:

- *Compression Washer/Ceramic Cartridge Faucet*
- *Ball Faucet*
- *Cartridge Faucet*
- *Ceramic Disk Faucet*

a. Fixing Ceramic and Compression Washer Faucets

Step 1: Pry off the decorative cap on the handle.

Step 2: Unscrew and remove the handle. If the handle is stuck you may need to use a handle puller tool, similar to a wheel puller used in automotive repairs. Try some penetrating release oil first.

Step 3: Underneath, you can find a packing nut which holds the stem to the faucet body. Use an adjustable wrench to remove the packing nut from below and pull out the stem. On some faucets you will need to rotate the stem out of the faucet. This will expose the O-ring and or the seat washer, which are the usual culprits for leaky faucets.

Step 4: Replace the O-ring and or seat washer with a new one. Now coat both of them with heatproof, nontoxic plumber's grease. Look at the seat the washer pushes against at the bottom of the tube where you removed the stem. If the seat is corroded or pitted it may be more effective to replace the entire faucet if the new washers do not correct the leak.

O-rings and seat washers vary in size. It is important to exactly match the size on your faucet.

Step 5: Re-assemble the faucet and tighten the packing nut, install the handle and turn on the water. The leak should now be fixed.

Compression water faucets and some ceramic cartridge faucets are easiest to identify as they have two handles, one for hot and one for cold.

b. Fixing Ball Faucets

Step 1: Purchase a washer replacement kit for your ball faucet. Replacement kits for ball faucets can be purchased from most hardware stores for about $20.00 USD. The replacement kit will include all the items and some tools that you will need to replace the faucet cam assembly, including instructions.

Step 2: Unscrew the set screw for the handle, pull off the handle and place it aside.

Step 3: Use pliers to remove the collar and cap. Wrap a rag around the collar and cap to help prevent scratching.

Step 4: Remove faucet cam, washer, and ball using the tools provided in the kit.

Step 5: Remove the springs and seals. This will expose the O-ring.

Step 6: Replace the old O-ring with a new one and then coat it with plumber's grease. O-rings vary in size. It is important to exactly match the size on your faucet. The repair kit may contain many different sized O-rings.

Step 7: Replace springs, valve seats, and cam washers with new ones that are included in the kit, replace the ball cam, then cap and make snug.

Step 8: Re-assemble the handle. Turn on water. The leak should now be fixed.

c. Fixing Cartridge Faucets

Step 1: Pry off the decorative cap. Unscrew the handle set screw and remove the handle by tilting it backwards and pulling off.

Step 2: Use pliers to remove the retaining cap, which is a circular threaded piece that holds the cartridge in place. Wrap the retainer cap with a rag to help prevent scratching.

Step 3: Pull the cartridge up. This is the position of the cartridge when the water is on full-blast.

Step 4: Remove the faucet spout. This will expose the O-ring(s).

Step 5: Pry or Cut off the old

O-ring using a knife. Coat a new O-ring with plumber's grease before installing. O-rings vary in size. It is important to exactly match the size on your faucet.

Step 6: Replace the old O-ring with a new one after coating it with plumber's grease.

Step 7: Replace springs, valve seats, and cam washers with new ones that are included in the kit and replace the cartridge.

Step 8: Reassemble the handle. Turn on the water. The leak should now be fixed.

In some cases if you can see the brand name on the faucet you may be able to take a photo of it and obtain the repair parts from the local hardware store prior to dismantling.

d. Fixing Ceramic-Disk Faucets

Step 1: Unscrew and remove the handle. Some have a set screw holding the handle in place.

Step 2: Locate and remove the escutcheon cap that sits directly beneath the handle. These may simply slide off or may be screwed on.

Step 3: Unscrew and remove the disk cylinder. This will expose neoprene seals.

Step 4: Remove the seals and place them along with the disk cylinder in a bowl containing white vinegar. Soak them for several hours in the bowl.

Step 5: Replace the seals with new ones if they look frayed, pitted, thin or otherwise worn. Ceramic-disc faucet seals vary in size. It is important to find the exact match at the hardware store. Knowing the brand of the faucet, if possible, will help locating the proper part much easier.

Step 6: Reassemble the handle and turn on the water. The leak should now be fixed.

1.4. GUTTER CLEANING & MAINTENANCE

A clogged gutter prevents rainwater from flowing away from your home. This will cause water to pool on the roof or near the house possibly damaging the foundation, or resulting in leakage into the house. Therefore, it is essential that the gutters are kept clean of dirt, leaves, twigs, and debris. You should make a habit of thoroughly cleaning your gutters every spring and fall, or after a windy period. Following this step-by-step guide will help you to clean your home gutter system using simple tools and accessories. You might consider installation of leaf guards to help prevent debris from entering the gutter in the first place.

Things You Will Need:
- A ladder tall enough to lean on the gutter and extend at least three feet past the top of the gutter. Never stand on the parts of the ladder marked "not a step" including the top of a stepladder
- Gutter Cleaning Tongs
- Trowel
- Garden Hose with Straight Nozzle
- 2 Buckets
- Wire Hooks
- Plumber's Snake Tool (If required: read step 4 below)
- Heavy gloves

1. Gutter Cleaning Tips

Step 1: After placing the ladder on a solid surface per the instructions on the ladder, begin cleaning debris near the downspout. Use a trowel to pick up the debris and place it in a bucket. Be careful, as there may be screw points and other hazards inside the gutter that can cut you.

Step 2: Don't reach. Move the ladder to access un-cleaned areas. Climb the ladder and use gutter-cleaning thongs to pick up debris from the roof gutter. Use a wire hook to attach a bucket to the ladder and place debris in the bucket so you always have at least one hand on the ladder. Repeat until the entire gutter is cleaned.

Step 3: Now, flush the gutter lengths using a hose to remove finer materials not removed with the trowel and tongs.

Step 4: If the gutter does not drain, the downspout may be clogged. In order to clean the downspout, follow these simple steps.

4a: Remove downspout from the pipe if it runs underground.

4b: Lock the hose nozzle at full pressure and feed the hose up from the bottom of the spout.

4c: If this doesn't clear the downspout, use a plumber's snake to clear the blockage.

4d: Reattach the downspout and flush the entire gutter again. If water spills out where the downspout connects to the underground pipe then the underground pipe is clogged.

Note: Use a firm ladder placed on a level, solid surface to clean your gutter. Avoid standing on top of the roof or placing your weight on the gutter due to risk of injury. Also, do not reach past the ladder side rail while standing on the ladder to avoid injury due to fall. This procedure has risk of personal injury and if you have any doubts contact a professional to perform this task.

2. Gutter Repair Tips

If water remains in the gutter after cleaning the debris, it may need repairs. The water may not drain due to gutter leaks, damage to the gutter sections or downspout, or improper slope. Here we will provide tips on repairing gutters to ensure that water drains freely without pooling in the gutter or on the roof.

3. Fixing Gutter Leaks

a) To repair leaks at the end caps: Run a bead of gutter sealant along the inside of the joints to repair leaks at the end caps. Be sure to clean the area to be sealed first.

b) To repair leaks at the seam: Add sealant on both sides of the joints (inside and out) to repair leaks at the seam or joint.

c) To repair holes in the gutter material: Purchase a gutter repair kit from your local hardware store. Before purchasing the kit, determine whether your gutter is made of aluminum or plastic/fiberglass material. In the kit, you can find aluminum or plastic/fiberglass patching compound. Apply this compound in the damaged area of the gutter following the instructions provided in the kit. Sometimes small holes can be repaired with silicone caulk type sealant. Budget for replacement if the gutters are badly deteriorated.

4. Repairing Damaged Gutter Hangers

All gutters are attached by different types of hangers. If the gutter hanger is damaged and cannot be bent back into shape you will need to replace it with a new one. Following these steps will help you in replacing damaged gutter hangers.

Step 1: Purchase the right type of hanger from the hardware store – it may be best to take a photograph of the existing hanger and bring that with you.

Step 2: Mark the position of the hanger on the gutter.

Step 3: Drill small pilot holes in the gutter lip and fascia to avoid damage. In the event you are using the same location as a previous hanger, a larger diameter and or longer spike/screw may be needed to be secure and not slide back out of the hole.

Step 4: Install the screw or the spike through the ferrule.

Step 5: Drive the screw with a drill or hammer the spike through the ferrule and install the hanger.

Note: Make sure that the hangers are spaced every 3-6 feet (.9M to 1.8M) along the gutter – plastic gutters require more hangers at tighter intervals, metal gutters can span farther. In the case where there is no fascia board to hold the hanger, you will need roof hangers with straps and follow package instruction to install the hangers.

5. Adjusting Slope of the Gutter

The gutter should be sloped correctly towards the downspout(s) to allow water to drain down the slope to the downspout opening. If it is not properly sloped, water may pool in the gutter. The gutter system should decline about 1 to 2-inches (2.5 to 3.0 CM) for every 10-foot (3M) toward the downspout. You can follow these steps to adjust slope of the gutter. This job is best done with two people, each with his own safely placed ladder.

Step 1: Detach the hangers that support your roof gutter, only detaching sections that can be managed by two people at a time. You may need to leave in place a few of the hangers in order to stabilize the gutter. Often only the hangers in the area not properly sloped need to be relocated.

Step 2: Adjust the gutter to ensure that it declines enough to allow water to flow towards and down the downspout opening. Note that some longer gutters may be equipped with a downspout at each end, with the gutter designed to slope to each downspout, generally from the middle of the gutter.

Step 3: Re-attach the gutter hangers making sure they are firmly in place.

Step 4: Flush the gutter using a water hose to check whether the water drains properly. Gutters are generally not sloped as much as plumbing drains to allow the water to drain slower. This prevents debris from being driven to the drain opening, potentially overloading the downspout.

1.5. PREVENT & THAW FROZEN PIPES

We rely on our plumbing to keep our homes comfortable. One of the major problems faced by many homeowners in northern parts of the U.S. and throughout Canada during winter is frozen pipes. Extremely low temperatures cause water inside the pipes to expand as it changes from liquid to solid – the freezing process. This may cause damage to the pipes due to increased pressure. Read on as we unveil the steps you will need to take to help prevent freezing of pipes. We will also show you how to thaw pipes if they become frozen.

1. How to Prevent Frozen Pipes

a.) Insulation of Water Pipes
You should insulate water pipes that are exposed to cold winds and snow during the winter season. This will prevent freezing of the water pipes during extreme cold temperatures. It is essential that the insulation is properly installed as even a small opening can allow cold air to get in and freeze a pipe. Polyethylene, fiberglass, or neoprene foams are the most common material used to insulate water pipes. Cold, combined with wind, is the most likely weather to cause frozen pipes. Most common locations where pipes freeze are: crawlspaces, attics, outside walls and under cantilevered (overhang) areas, in particular bathrooms that overhang the first floor, or are above an unheated garage.

b.) Install Heat Tape to Prevent Frozen Pipes
Another way to prevent freezing of pipes is to install a heat tape to vulnerable areas. To install heat tape, you need to determine the size and length of pipe that needs to be protected from cold weather. Determining the proper length is important so the heat tape is neither too long nor too short as most should not be wrapped upon themselves.

Installing heat tape is a cost effective but usually temporary solution to prevent frozen pipes. The reason it is not a permanent solution to prevent frozen pipes is that the heat tape deteriorates over time, and will cease to function. You should regularly check the heat tape to ensure that it has not worn out, and is operating; otherwise it may cause the pipes to freeze and burst. Proper placement of pipes deep underground or in heated areas is the best protection for frozen pipes.

c.) Keep Faucets Running at Slow Drip
Another temporary solution, usually only done during very cold and windy weather, to prevent frozen pipes is to keep the faucets running at a slow drip. This will keep the water moving which will prevent freezing of water inside the pipes. You can catch the dripping water inside with buckets and recycle it to use for cleaning purposes or watering the plants if you desire – but don't forget to check the buckets regularly – they fill up fast.

Note: Polyethylene, fiberglass, or neoprene foams are the most common material used to insulate water pipes.

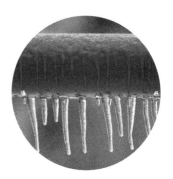

d.) Install Hot Water Re-circulating Pump

You can also install a retro-fit water re-circulating pump at remote sink(s) to prevent freezing of pipes. The re-circulating pump has a sensor that activates when the water in the pipes becomes cold, or it can be set to operate during the entire cold season. It pumps cool water back to the water heater which is replaced with warm water, and then turns off automatically when the temperature reaches a preset point, or some work by timer.

The circulator pump constantly circulates a small amount of hot water through the pipes. Water circulates from the heater to the fixture where the pump is located and back to the heater. This ensures that hot water is not wasted down the drain and prevents freezing of water inside the pipes. This system will cause your water heater to heat somewhat more often; however, this is generally much less costly than repairing frozen pipes.

e.) Use a Space Heater

Space heaters can also be used to prevent freezing of pipes. The space heater is installed near cold weather exposed water pipes. This ensures that the unprotected water pipes do not freeze during extremely cold weather. Most space heaters have a thermostat so the heater will operate automatically at a preset temperature. Most experts recommend setting temperatures at least 50 F (10 C) to compensate for wind chill from drafts if needed.

2. How to Thaw Frozen Pipes

Frozen water pipes are common during winter seasons. If you turn on the tap and the water does not come out or flows slowly, frozen water pipes may be the cause. This is a cause for concern because frozen water can rupture or burst the pipe, which may not leak until unfrozen.

It is important that you follow proper procedures in thawing pipes. Here are some of the steps that you can take to thaw frozen pipes.

Step 1: Open the faucet(s) that are blocked. This will allow vapor produced by your thawing activity to escape from the faucet and you can monitor to figure out when the pipe is un-thawed.

Step 2: Now you have to determine which pipe is frozen. You should look for exposed portions of your plumbing you might find in the attic, basement, crawlspace, outside wall or outside of your house, or consider where wind may have driven cold air near a pipe inside the house. Note, if only certain fixtures are not working the freezing is probably isolated to the branch feeding this location.

Step 3: You can use either a hair dryer or a heat gun to thaw the pipe. Turn the hair dryer or the heat gun to the highest setting and slowly wave the device back and forth starting from the end of frozen section of the pipe. Note that if you start thawing in the middle section of the frozen pipe, steam could get trapped in the middle and burst the pipe. If the pipes are plastic be careful not to melt or burn the pipe.

Step 4: As the ice melts, steam and water, possibly containing ice chunks, will come out of the open faucet.

Note: You can also wrap warm towels or electrical heat tape around frozen sections of the pipes for thawing.

In some cases, the water pipes behind the interior wall of the house may freeze. This may happen during extreme frigid weather when the house is not provided with adequate heat. If this is the case, you should follow these steps to thaw frozen wall pipe.

Step 1: Open the faucet(s) that are blocked.

Step 2: Activate and turn up the heat in the house to around 75°F - 80°F (24-27 C) and wait for 2 to 3 hours. Water will start dripping from the faucet as the ice melts.

Step 3: Constantly check for leaks as it is a possibility that some of the pipes have burst and are leaking. If so, turn off the water main, and call a plumber. If you have hot water type heat there is a possibility that some of the heat pipes have frozen and may leak as well.

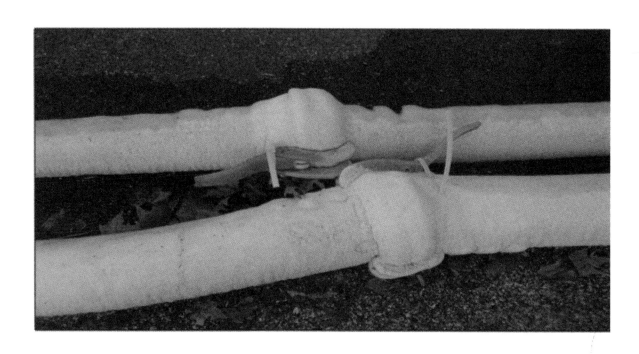

1.6. DEALING WITH CLOGGED TOILETS

Clogs may happen at the most inopportune time. A clogged toilet can flood the bathroom and create a very unpleasant situation. Fortunately, it can be very easy to fix clogged toilets. Many times you do not need to call and wait for a plumper to repair a clogged toilet. Just follow these simple, easy-to-follow instructions to get rid of this bathroom nuisance within minutes.

Things You Will Need:
- Plunger
- Plumber's Snake
- Rubber Gloves
- Old towels for mess cleanup

Step 1: Put on a pair of gloves and press the plunger into the bowl slowly but firmly. Make sure the plunger covers the hole completely and is submerged in the water.

Step 2: Push the plunger in and out of the bowl vigorously. Repeat this step until the toilet becomes unclogged. Be careful as plunging tends to spray water out of the bowl. You might want to place old towels around the bottom of the toilet bowl.

Step 3: If the plunging drains the bowl but the toilet is still clogged, leave the plunger in the bowl, and fill the bowl with water over the top of the plunger bulb. Then plunge again several times until the toilet becomes unclogged. Be sure to have the tank lid removed when testing if the toilet is unclogged so you can manually close the flapper if necessary to prevent flooding.

If the plunger does not unclog the toilet, you have to use a plumber's snake (also called a toilet auger). A plumber's snake is a long wire coil with a corkscrew-like tip contained in a long handle that has a bend at the bottom end. Most plumbers use a snake to unclog toilets.
Step 1: Insert one end of the plumber's snake into the drain. Push the plumber's snake through the bowl drain curves while slowly rotating the handle clockwise until you feel an obstruction.

Step 2: Twist and push the plumber's snake until the obstruction clears and water begins to drain.

Step 3: Slowly pull the snake from the drain. You may need to turn it counter-clockwise during removal. It is wise to clean the snake while removing with a rag, and be ready to grab the tip to prevent the debris from spraying.

1.7. HOW TO UNCLOG SINKS

A clogged sink is another plumbing problem faced by home-owners. It is usually caused by a buildup of gunk, dirt, or hair in the sink drain, many times at the drain stopper. You can follow these steps to unclog sinks in your kitchen or bathroom.

Things You Will Need:
- Plunger
- Plumber's Snake
- Rubber Gloves

Step 1: Fill the sink with hot water. If the sink has an overflow opening, or it is a kitchen sink and the dishwasher drain has an air gap device on the sink top, you may need to have someone hold a wet rag over the overflow opening or air gap device, and the other sink bowl drain opening if a double bowl sink, to prevent the water exiting due to the plunger creating pressure in the line. Pressure is how the plunger works.

Step 2: Position a plunger over the drain and be sure there is water over the bell end of the plunger.

Also be sure to remove any sink drain stopper device prior to plunging.

Step 3: Work the plunger up and down quickly. Pull the plunger off the drain opening to see if the water starts to drain. Repeat the process until the clog is dislodged. Be sure to check under the sink for any leaks once completed.

Note: In the event the plunger does not unclog the drain, you may have to use a plumber's snake. Twist clockwise and push the plumber's snake into the drain until the obstruction clears and the water begins to drain. Often it is easier to remove the trap under the sink and insert the snake into the wall fitting. Be sure to clean any hair and debris from the sink stopper in a lavatory sink. Many times this debris is the cause of the slow draining.

1.8. HOW TO FIX REDUCED WATER FLOW

Water flow adequacy problems are common at bathroom sinks. Sometimes when you turn on the faucet, the water barely trickles out of the tap. There are a number of reasons for a slow water stream from the faucet. Identifying the cause of low water flow is the first step in repairing it.

Some of the possible causes of reduced water flow include:
- Debris in the water which clogs faucets
- Mineral deposit build-up inside pipes or faucets
- Water leaks relieving pressure thus taking away the "push" behind the water
- Faulty pressure reducing valve
- Low water pressure from the city or inadequate water in the private well
- Valve under the sink not fully opened

1. Debris in the Water/Pipes

The most common cause of low water flow is debris in the water and pipes in the house and or the feeder pipe to the house. If your house has galvanized iron pipes, they rust with time and can plug up the aerators and valves. Often the pipes themselves have restricted interiors due to rust and mineral buildup. Sometimes the plastic "dip tube" pipe inside the water heater may disintegrate and pieces of plastic float in the water. This may also restrict water flow, although usually only at some faucets. To solve the problem of debris in water, you have to locate the source of the rust or other debris and replace water lines to eliminate the problem. It is common to re-pipe homes with galvanized water piping as generally they were installed prior to the 1960's and have served their normal useful life. If the debris is coming from the source of water, it is possible filtering will trap most of the debris.

2. Mineral Deposit Build-up

Mineral build-up can also restrict water flow in the pipes. Water that has high deposits of mineral is called hard water. Water hardness is measured in GPG or grains of mineral per gallon. Water that tests at 3.5 GPG or above is considered hard water. Hard water that is caused due to mineral deposits creates buildup, reacts with some cleaning products, and damages fixtures and appliances like dishwashers quickly.

The solution for treating hard water is to install a water softener or other treatment system in the house. You should select a water softener based on GPG hardness of the water per the manufacturer's instructions. The water softener comes with a bypass valve, or the installer places one in the inlet/outlet piping. This allows you to shut off the water going through the water softener while still maintaining water service to the house, in case you want to redirect the water for any reason or the unit malfunctions and needs service. It is best to consult with a water treatment professional for hard water treatment and a system that best suits your needs and meets local requirements, if any.

Note: The solution for treating hard water is to install a water softener or other treatment system in the house. You should select a water softener based on GPG hardness of the water per the manufacturer's instructions.

3. Water Leaks

Water leaks can also result in reduced water flow in homes. You have to identify the source of water leaks to fix the problem. The steps required to identify water leaks in the home are described in the section "Diagnosing Water Leaks at Home". Once the source of water leaks is identified, you have to eliminate water leaks to resolve the issue.

4. Faulty Water Pressure Regulating Valve

A pressure regulator is a bell shaped device that regulates water pressure in the home, usually to lower it from high street pressure. It is usually located near the main shut off valve or below the hose connection in front of the home. It may be located in other areas as well.

If the water pressure regulator is not working properly, it may reduce water supply in the home. Replacing a water pressure valve is a medium intensity project. Here are some of the steps required to fix a faulty water pressure valve.

Step 1: Close the water valve off to the house. Sometimes you may need a special "curb key" to turn off the valve near the street.

Step 2: Empty water lines as much as possible by opening several faucets - both hot and cold water – the lowest ones are the best for this task.

Step 3: Squeeze some penetrating solvent onto the threaded union connection of the water pressure regulator. This will help loosen the connection.

Step 4: Place a water bucket under the water pressure regulator to collect any water left in the lines. At times this can be a substantial amount, possibly several gallons/liters.

Step 5: Adjust one of the pipe wrenches to keep the pipe connection fitting from twisting. Now fix another wrench to the large nut going to the regulator. Hold the pipe in place and loosen the large nut with the wrench.

Step 6: Remove the pressure regulator by rotating the regulator itself off the pipe fitting, or another nut type fitting.

Step 7: Wrap Teflon sealant tape around the male threaded connections on the plumbing and on the new water pressure valve.

Step 8: Install the new regulator in place of the old water pressure regulator and tighten the connections. Make sure to hold the pipe in place with a wrench to avoid damaging the pipes. If possible, purchasing the same brand of pressure regulating valve makes

Note: Some pressure regulators do not have a locknut union type connection and may require soldering or other professional service to install. When in doubt always call a professional.

swap-out easy due to similar dimensions and threads.

Step 9: Close the opened faucets and turn the water back on. Inspect and tighten the connection if necessary. Open a hose faucet valve at the opposite end of the house from the pressure regulator first to bleed off air and any debris in the lines, then open and run each inside faucet fixture to bleed off the air until water only runs without "burping".

Step 10: Adjust the pressure setting on the new regulator according to the manufacturer's instructions. Generally a pressure around 60 PSI (.413 MPa) is recommended. You may need a water pressure gauge for this task.

5. Low Water Pressure from the Municipal Supply

Finally, low water pressure from the municipal source (AKA "city water") can also cause reduced water flow at faucets. Oftentimes when the pressure at the street is low, and the house is located much higher than the source, the pressure is not adequate to "push" sufficient water to the faucets. One solution to the problem is to install a pressure booster pump and tank system to normalize water pressure. Another solution may be to install a bigger water service pipe and piping inside the home to increase flow.

The Uniform Plumbing Code is a model code developed by IAPMO (International Association of Plumbing and Mechanical Officials) to govern plumbing systems in homes. The UPC includes pipe sizing tables, including one for lower water pressure. For low municipal pressure, it is best to consult a professional as generally a booster system is needed which must be sized and installed properly to be effective.

1.9. SHOWER AND TUB ENCLOSURE CLEANING AND MAINTENANCE

Shower enclosures can get mold, soap scum, and grime buildup over time. Daily care and weekly cleaning will prevent buildup and help keep the tub enclosure sparkling clean. Here are a few guidelines to help prevent buildup of deposits on shower and tub enclosures as well as how to clean them.

1. Tips to Prevent Buildup on Shower and Tub Enclosure

Tip 1: Prevent mold and mineral buildup from taking hold by wiping the walls after each shower. A squeegee works well for this task. Start at the top and sweep downwards.

Tip 2: Leave the shower door open to allow air to circulate and dry the enclosure. This helps prevent buildup of mold on the shower or tub enclosure. If your bathroom has an exhaust fan or window, turn on the fan or open the window during use to allow moisture to escape.

Tip 3: Spray the shower area with mildew inhibitor or disinfectant to prevent the buildup of mold (it really is mold in the shower, mildew only occurs outside on plants).

Tip 4: Coat the tile walls of your shower area with furniture polish. This will help prevent soap scum buildup and water spots.

2. Guide to Cleaning Shower and Tub Enclosures

Tip 1: To clean hard water deposits on shower enclosures: Use a solution of water and white vinegar. Spray the affected areas, wait 15 minutes, scrub and wash down.

Tip 2: To loosen and clean soap scum from shower doors: Add 1-cup liquid fabric softener to 1-quart warm water and use it to wipe soap scum off with a sponge. You can also add 1 part mineral oil with 4 parts water to clean soap scum off the shower walls.

Tip 3: To remove water spots on metal frames around shower doors: Scrub the area with lemon oil.

Tip 4: To remove buildup of mineral deposits on shower walls: Use vinegar and an abrasive scrubbing pad – only for glazed tile. You can also use a toothbrush to remove buildup deposits around tub fixtures. If the enclosure is fiberglass

Note:
Never use harsh abrasive powders or steel-wool pads to wipe deposits off the shower and tub enclosure. It may damage the bathroom fixtures. You should spray the shower and tub area with all-purpose bathroom cleaner, and allow the product to stand for a few minutes. The cleaning product will dissolve oil and soap scum, so you will need less scrubbing to remove the deposits

or plastic do not use an abrasive pad. Use a sponge and white vinegar in water, rinsing when done.

Tip 5: To remove a ring around the tub: Scrub the area with a nylon mesh ball or pad. Stubborn bathtub rings can be cleaned with a paste of cream of tartar and hydrogen peroxide.

Tip 6: To remove rust stains in shower enclosure: Use commercial rust removers. Be sure to wear rubber gloves when using rust removers as they may contain acid. Some homeowners have reported a mixture of vinegar and baking soda works well for enamel, vinegar and dish soap for fiberglass.

Tip 7: To clean discolored porcelain fixtures: Wipe off the area with a paste made of cream of tartar moistened with hydrogen peroxide. You can also use a paste of borax moistened with lemon juice.

Tip 8: To remove yellowed discoloration of enameled bathtubs: Rub the area with a solution of turpentine and salt, and rinse well. Remember to wear rubber gloves when working with this solution and ventilate the area well, a fan will help move the air.

CHAPTER 2: HVAC AND WATER HEATER MAINTENANCE & REPAIR

2.1. TROUBLESHOOTING WATER HEATER PROBLEMS

Water heaters are familiar fixtures in most homes. Not many people like a cold shower. A water heater warms the water and ensures continuous delivery of hot water, if sized properly.

There are two types of energy sources for water heaters in most homes - gas water heaters and electric water heaters. They can be storage tank type or tankless. Some may be supplemented by solar panels, or heat from a hot water boiler. Regardless of what type of water heater is installed in your home, the following troubleshooting guide will help you in resolving issues with your water heater.

1. Gas Water Heater Problems

Troubleshooting gas water heaters is basically a process of elimination. If your gas water heater has stopped working, you can follow these steps to determine the cause of the problem and resolve the issue.

a) No Hot Water
If the gas water heater does not heat the water, it may be due to one or more of the following:

Possible Causes:
*   Gas pilot not lit - Check gas pilot flame and pilot operation. See How to Light a Gas Appliance Pilot for more information.
*   Faulty gas thermocouple - Retighten, reposition, or replace gas valve thermocouple. See How to replace gas thermocouple for more information.
*   Faulty gas pilot control valve - Replace the gas pilot control valve. Call a professional to do this task for you as it requires special tools and knowledge.
*   Gas Off - Check cut off valve at heater, check gas meter or gas tank.

b) Inadequate Hot Water
If the gas water heater provides inadequate hot water, it may be due to one or more of the following:

Possible Causes:
*   Water heater unit is undersized for water heating demand - Spread out hot water usage or replace water heater with proper sized unit.

CAUTION!

Make Sure the Gas Is OFF before you start troubleshooting your gas water heater if you smell gas. It is best to contact your local gas supplier or plumbing professional if you believe there is a gas leak.

- Faulty Thermostat - Replace gas control valve if the thermostat is out of order. Call a professional to do this task for you.
- Clogged Burner orifice - Remove and clean clogged burner orifice. Call a professional to do this task for you.
- Broken or damaged water heater dip tube - Remove dip tube and check for cracks or breakage. See How to install water heater dip tube for more information.
- Sediment Deposit - An extreme amount of sediment at the bottom of the tank may result in an inadequate water supply as the sediment insulates the burner from the water in the tank. You should drain and flush the water heater per manufacturer instructions to resolve the issue. It is best to call a professional to do this task for you when the sediment is extreme.
- Low gas pressure - Call the gas supplier to resolve the issue.
- Faulty plumbing - The problem may also be caused by crossed cold and hot water connections. Turn off the water supply to the heater and open a hot water faucet. If the water comes out, then there is a crossed connection somewhere. Check for a hot water line connected to a cold-water connection on the water heater or appliances such as dishwasher, washer, shower valves, or faucets as cool water could be back-feeding into the hot water supply line. This is a rare condition, but still found occasionally.

c) Rust Colored Water

If rust colored water comes out of the hot water, it could be caused by any of the following:

Possible Causes
- Corrosion inside the glass lined tank - When the sacrificial anode rod dissolves, it results in corrosion inside the tank and then the corrosive minerals will attack the tank. You should replace the anode rod with a new anode to solve the problem. See How to replace anode rod for more information.

d) Rotten Smell

If the water that comes out of the hot water tap smells of rotten eggs, it is likely due to bacteria in the tank that is created from decay of the sacrificial anode. This usually only occurs after a long period of non-use of the heater. Here are some of the steps you can take to resolve the problem.

- Flush the water heater per manufacturer instructions. This usually entails connecting a hose to the tank drain and allowing it to drain.
- Treat tank and water in lines with 2 pints of hydrogen peroxide solution (3% peroxide mixed in 40 gallons of water). Let the solution sit in the tank and pipes for 2 hours. The solution is non- toxic and requires no rinsing. You will need to create an access to the tank to introduce the hydrogen peroxide. Most plumbers will remove the cold water connection pipe to accomplish this task.
- Another method is to superheat the tank to kill the bacteria. Try turning the thermostat all the way up for half an hour, then reduce the temperature back to the original setting. Do not forget to return the ther-

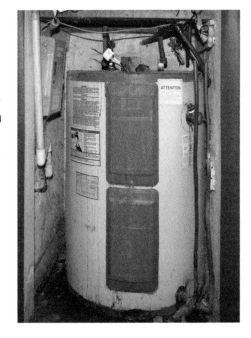

mostat to the proper position to prevent scalding.

- Replace the anode with a zinc-alloy anode if the problem persists.

e) Leak Around Base of Heater

If the water leaks around base of the heater, it can be caused by any of the following:

Possible Causes

- Leaking water tank due to corrosion - If the tank is leaking you need a new water heater. This job is best performed by a professional, as most jurisdictions require a permit.

T&P (Temperature & Pressure) relief valve leak due to overheating, excessive pressure --- Reduce thermostat temperature to avoid overheating. Open the T&P valve to flush debris and reduce excess pressure in the water lines. You may need to have thermal expansion controls installed, such as an expansion tank, if this condition persists.

- Faulty T&P (temperature and pressure) relief valve - Replace T&P valve if it is faulty. See How to replace T&P (Temperature & Pressure) valve for more information.
- Leak from nearby or overhead plumbing connection - The leak may also be caused due to leaks from nearby or overhead plumbing pipes or connections. Fix the leaky plumbing pipes or valves to resolve the problem.
- Faulty Water Heater - The leak in the water heater tank may also be caused by heavy rusting or accumulation of water in the combustion chamber. In this case you need to replace the water heater. Many times

this indicates improper venting and the gas flue should be checked.

f) Water is Too Hot or Cold

If the water is too hot or cold, it could be caused by any of the following:

Possible Causes

- Thermostat Settings - If your hot water system has a storage tank, you should set the thermostat to 50° - 55°C (120°F - 130°F). If you have a tankless water heater, set the thermostat to 50°C (122°F). Under no circumstances should the delivery temperature at the faucet spouts exceed 50°C (122° F).
- Faulty Thermostat - Replace the thermostat if the temperature settings are out of order. It is best to call a professional to do this task for you.

2. Electric Water Heater Problems

Electric water heaters use electric power directed to immersion elements rather than a gas flame to heat the water. In the case your electric water heater has malfunctioned, you should check the previous section relating to gas water heaters to help resolve the problem – some of the issues can be the same in either type heater. If the problem is not resolved, the following may help you to solve the problem.

a) Water is Too Hot or Cold

A tripped or faulty circuit breaker may result in insufficient power fed to the water heater. You should reset the circuit breaker to solve the problem. If the circuit breaker trips again after being reset, it may need replacement or

there may be an internal problem with the heater. If the water is too hot, generally this is caused by a faulty or improperly set thermostat. Note, some electric heaters have two thermostats, one at the upper element, and the other at the lower.

b) Faulty Water Heating Element

With electric heaters, most often the bottom heating element will fail first, as it is the one that does most of the work. If the heating element is faulty, you should contact a plumber to resolve the issue.

CAUTION!

Make sure that the water heater power is off before troubleshooting the water heater. Shut off all breakers until you have determined which one shuts off the electric water heater if the individual breaker is not labeled. Most electric water heaters should have a dedicated power disconnect within sight of the heater.

2.2. HOW TO LIGHT A GAS APPLIANCE PILOT

The gas furnace, gas water heater, or other gas appliance pilot light serves as a small ignition flame for the main gas burner. When this small ignition flame does not work properly or goes out, the gas appliance cannot function. In older style heaters, the pilot light is lit with a match or lighter. The access panel for the pilot orifice is located at the bottom of the tank in the case of a gas water heater. Newer models have a sealed burner compartment and the pilot is lit with a push button spark generator (usually red).

Here's how you re-light your gas appliance pilot for both the old and new model water heaters (and other gas appliances as well).

---

1. Lighting Older Style Water Heaters

Step 1: Rotate the temperature control knob until it is set to the lowest setting.

Step 2: Turn the mode control knob to the "pilot" setting. Most have three settings' "off", "pilot" and "on".

Step 3: Take out both the inner and outer burner access panels. These normally pull up and out and are held in place with metal tabs.

Step 4: Press down and hold the "pilot" button. In some models the on/off control knob itself is pressed when it is set on pilot.

Step 5: Now, light the pilot with a long snout lighter or match near the main burner at the end of the smaller silver tube coming out of the bottom of the gas control valve. This is the pilot supply tube and at the end of this tube is the pilot light area.

Step 6: After the pilot is lit, you should continue to hold the pilot button for another 20 - 30 seconds to warm the thermocouple. Now, slowly release the button. If the pilot light goes out, light it again and hold the button down for a little longer. If the pilot light does not stay lit after a few tries, most likely the thermocouple is defective and needs replacement.

Step 7: Replace both the inner and outer access panels. Turn the control knob to the "on" setting and set the temperature dial to the desired setting. You should be able to see and/or hear the flame at the burner fire up. If the pilot flame will not stay lit when you release the button, most likely the thermocouple is defective, which is best replaced by a professional.

2. Lighting a Newer Style Water Heater

Step 1: Rotate the temperature control knob until it is set to the lowest setting.

Step 2: Turn the control knob to the "pilot" setting.

Step 3: Press down and hold the "pilot" button.

CAUTION!

If you smell gas, wait 15 minutes before attempting to light the pilot. If the smell of gas persists, contact your local gas supplier immediately.

CAUTION!

Do not fire the burner while the access panels are off.

Step 4: Slowly press the spark generator button while looking through the sight glass until you hear it click, holding it down for a few seconds.

Step 5: You should see a spark from the generator and the pilot light should light. After the pilot is lit, you should hold the pilot button down for 20 - 30 seconds to allow the thermocouple to get hot before releasing the button.

Step 6: If the pilot does not light, it may be due to air in the line. To resolve the problem, press the spark generator button every 10 seconds while holding the pilot button down. You should keep pressing the generator button until the pilot lights. If this does not work after 4-6 attempts the unit probably needs in-depth troubleshooting by a professional.

Step 7: Turn the control knob to the "on" setting and set the temperature to the desired setting. You should be able to see the flame through the site glass and hear the burner fire up.
If after lighting the pilot light it won't stay lit, you should follow these steps to resolve the issue.

3. Pilot Will Not Light

Possible Causes
- Gas Off - Check shut off valve at the gas supply to the appliance, check gas meter, and check gas tank.
- Air in gas line - Hold pilot button down and try to relight several times.
- Clogged Burner Orifice - Remove and clean clogged burner orifice. It is best to call a professional to do this task for you.
- Pilot supply line kinked or clogged - Check if the supply line is defective – Replace if needed.
- Gas control valve defective - Replace gas conol valve if it is out of order. It is best to call a professional to do this task for you.

4. Pilot Lights but Will Not Stay Lit

Possible Causes
- Faulty thermocouple - Ensure that the tip of the thermocouple probe is in the pilot flame. Also make sure that the thermocouple locknut is tight at the gas control valve. Finally, check the thermocouple for problems and replace it if it is out of order. A defective thermocouple is the most common cause of a pilot light not staying lit. See How to replace gas appliance thermocouple for more information.
- Gas control valve defective - Replace gas control valve if it is out of order. It is best to call a professional to do this task for you.

5. Pilot Light Goes Out Intermittently

Possible Causes
- Faulty thermocouple - Ensure that the tip of the thermocouple probe is in the pilot flame. Also make sure that the thermocouple locknut is tight at the gas control valve. Finally check thermocouple for problems, replace it if it is out of order. See How to replace gas appliance thermocouple for more information.
- Clogged Burner or Pilot tube Orifice - Remove and clean clogged burner orifice. It is best to call a professional to do this task for you.
- Down draft - This may happen on very windy days, or there could be a draft into the appliance enclosure that is extinguishing the pilot flame.
- Gas control valve defective - Replace gas control valve it it has malfunctioned. It is best to call a professional to do this task for you.

2.3. HOW TO REPLACE A GAS FURNACE OR OTHER APPLIANCE THERMOCOUPLE AND FLAME SENSOR

Gas appliances, including furnaces, have thermocouples which control the flow of gas from the gas valve. A flame sensor performs the same task in electronic ignition appliances. The thermocouple and flame sensing rods connect to the gas valve or to the electronic control box and are generally part of a pilot burner. The thermocouple or flame sensor tells the main gas valve that the pilot light is lit, therefore it can open the main burner gas as that is the source of ignition. You should replace the thermocouple or flame sensor if the pilot light of your furnace won't stay lit.

1. Thermocouple Replacement

Step 1: Purchase a thermocouple that is compatible with your gas appliance – including proper length.

Step 2: Shut off gas to the appliance and remove the burner access cover.

Step 3: The thermocouple is screwed into the gas control valve and fastened to the pilot burner assembly at the burner with a nut at the bottom of the bracket, or sometimes as a pressure fit. You should unscrew the nuts and remove the thermocouple, or simply pull it out of the bracket.

Step 4: Now, pop the new thermocouple in the hole in the bracket. Make sure that the steel sensor tube is up while the copper lead is down. Reinstall nut if one were removed. Unscrew the old thermocouple locknut where it connects to the gas valve.

Step 5: Screw the locknut on the new thermocouple tube while pushing the connection nut into the female threaded connection where the copper lead connects to the gas valve.

Step 6: Turn on the gas to the appliance and turn on/light the pilot light. Make certain that ¼" to 1/2" (6-12 MM) of the thermocouple is in the pilot flame. Re-install the burner access covers.

2. Flame Sensor Replacement

Step 1: Purchase a new flame sensing rod that is compatible with your electronic ignition appliance.

Step 2: Shut off power and gas to the appliance.

Step 3: The sensor may be removed and fastened to the burner assembly with a screw. It may also be an integral part of the gas ignition system.

Step 4: If the sensor is removable, remove the electrical wire leads to the sensor. You should also disconnect the other end of the leads at the control box.

Step 5: Using the appropriate tool, loosen the fasteners and remove the flame sensor.

Step 6: Now, install the new flame sensor and secure it with the fasteners.

Step 7: Reconnect the electrical wire leads to the sensor. You should also connect the other end of the electrical leads to the electronic control box. Re-install the access covers. Activate the appliance and test for operation. If the unit does not operate properly it may be best to contact a professional to troubleshoot and repair the unit.

Note: Do not over tighten the bracket and connection nuts – you are not sealing fuel gas but rather holding the tube in place. Also, if the gas appliance has been operating, wait 30 minutes or more until the thermocouple cools prior to replacing.

2.4. HOW TO REPLACE WATER HEATER ANODE ROD FOR MAXIMUM SERVICE LIFE

Inside most residential water heaters is a long metal rod called a sacrificial "Anode Rod". This rod is typically made of aluminum, magnesium, zinc or a combination of these metals. The rod protects the lining of your heater's tank from corrosion by attracting the corrosive minerals. Eventually the rod will dissolve from these corrosive minerals and will no longer be able to protect your water heater tank from damage.

The life expectancy of anode rods is four to six years. You may extend the life of your water heater by replacing the anode rod in your water heater with a new one. Here are the steps you need to take to check and replace your water heater anode rod.

Step 1: Turn off gas / power to the water heater.

Step 2: Close the cold water shut-off valve and open a hot water tap. This will allow the pressure inside the tank to deplete.

Step 3: In order to clear any remaining water from the hot water pipes, you should draw off a few gallons of water through the heater drain valve until the water is below the anode rod access opening, normally at the top of the water heater tank. It will look like a hex pipe plug but flat at the top. Some heaters will have it clearly labeled.

Step 4: On top or sometimes the side of the water heater (usually the smaller units), you can view the threaded lug end of the anode rod. You may have to pry off a plastic cap first. Using a wrench or large socket and breaker bar, turn it counter clockwise until it clears the thread.

Step 5: Now carefully remove the anode rod. In some cases you may need to bend the anode if there is a ceiling or other obstruction. Inspect the rod for corrosion. Some surface corrosion is normal. However, if large pieces of the anode rod are missing or corroded, or all you see is a stiff wire, then you should replace the anode rod. The anode rod is generally about three feet or so (1 Meter) long so if there is a ceiling above you may need to purchase a sectional anode rod so you can bend it.

Step 6: You should purchase a new anode rod that is compatible with your water heater model. Once purchased you should reinstall the rod by first wrapping the threads in Teflon tape and carefully sliding the rod back into the hole. Make sure to tighten it securely.

Note: Sometimes these are very tight and having someone hold the heater while turning may prevent damage to plumbing pipes.

2.5 HOW TO FLUSH A WATER HEATER

Over time sediments minerals and other debris start to accumulate at the bottom of the water heater tank. These sediment deposits impair performance of the water heater and shorten its lifespan. Flushing the water heater is the only solution to remove sediment from the bottom of the tank. You should flush your water heater annually to remove sediment buildup inside the tank. Most manufacturers have flushing details in their instructions. Tankless water heaters also require flushing which is performed with a mild acid solution and is best left to a professional. If your tankless water heater does not have a flush kit installed, one will be needed the first time it is flushed.

Step 1: Shut off gas / electric power to the water heater. For a gas heater simply turning the control dial to "pilot" position will suffice.

Step 2: Turn off the cold water supply to the heater. Open a nearby hot water tap and leave it open. This will allow air to enter the tank as it empties.

Step 3: Connect a garden hose to the drain valve located near the bottom of the water heater. Make sure that the hose is long enough to reach a drain or area that will not harm plants with the warm water.

Step 4: Open the drain valve by using a flathead screwdriver. You have to turn the screw driver counter-clockwise to open the pipe unless the drain is equipped with a handle similar to a hose faucet.

Step 5: You should let the water drain from the heater, occasionally turning the cold water supply back on for 10 seconds or so to stir up and remove sediment from the tank. This should only take about five to ten minutes as there is no need to entirely drain the tank.

Step 6: Once the water heater has been completely flushed (water at the hose runs clear), you can refill the tank by closing the drain valve and turning the water supply back on. Do not turn on the power or light the burner until the tank is completely filled. You will know the tank is filled when water and no air comes from the faucet that was left open, which can now be closed.

CAUTION!

You should wait until the water cools down before flushing your water heater, which may take several hours.

2.6. HOW TO INSTALL WATER HEATER DIP TUBE

A faulty water heater dip tube can result in water heating problems (water gets cold fast) and pieces of plastic clogging the faucets. The water heater dip tube is a plastic pipe that travels vertically from the cold-water inlet to near the bottom of the tank. This tube brings cold water towards the bottom of the tank where it is heated. If the dip tube is broken or cracked, the cold water immediately mixes with hot water dilutes the hot water toward the top of the tank, or the cold water immediately exits the heater before being warmed. It is relatively easy to diagnose and replace a water heater dip tube. If you suspect that the dip tube of your water heater is broken, you should proceed with the following steps.

Step 1: Turn off gas/power to the water heater. For gas heaters turning the control to "pilot" position will suffice. Also, close the cold water shut off valve located just above the water heater.

Step 2: Connect a hose and open the heater drain valve in order to clear any remaining water from the hot water pipes above the level of the top of the tank.

Step 3: Disconnect the water supply flexible connector. Remove the nipple from the top of the heater - a short piece of pipe threaded at both ends - to expose the top of the water heater dip tube.

Step 4: Pry the white plastic tube out of the opening by using a screwdriver or your finger. You should hold the screwdriver at an angle to pull out the dip tube.

Step 5: If the dip tube is intact then the water heater problem may be due to other issues. However, if you find that the dip tube is missing large chunks or is heavily corroded, then you should install a new dip tube.

Step 6: Wrap the threads of the new dip tube fitting with Teflon tape. Now, put the dip tube into the water heater and replace the piping. Some dip tubes simply drop in and are not threaded.

Step 7: Finally, refill the hot water tank by opening the cold water supply, turn off the faucet you opened when water and no air exits, then turn on power/gas to the water heater.

Note: Some heaters may have the supply pipe connected by soldered copper pipes. Other times there is not sufficient space above the heater to replace the dip tube (about 3-feet or so, [1 Meter] long) and the heater will need to be disconnected and tipped to the side. In these cases it may be best to contact a professional, as special tools are needed.

2.7. HOW TO REPLACE A T&P (TEMPERATURE AND PRESSURE) RELIEF VALVE

Water heaters have a small valve screwed into the tank. The purpose of this valve is to relieve high temperature and pressure that builds up when the water heater overheats. This valve prevents the tank from exploding. The pressure function also protects the tank from high water pressure caused by faulty regulators or thermal expansion.

This valve is known as the Temperature and Pressure relief valve or simply T&P valve. As T&P valves get old, they may begin to leak and need to be replaced. You can easily buy a T&P valve from most hardware stores.

You should periodically check the valve to ensure that it is in good condition. If the valve begins to leak, then you should replace it as soon as possible. Some manufacturers recommend testing of the T&P valve, however, if you do so, be prepared to replace the valve if it does not turn back off. Often as these valves age the seats become corroded and may leak.

Here are the steps for replacing a T&P valve on a water heater.

Step 1: Turn off power (electricity or gas) to the water heater and set the temperature dial to its lowest setting. Also, shut off water supply to the water heater. For a gas unit simply setting the control to the "pilot" setting should suffice.

Step 2: Drain water pressure from the tank by opening the lowest hot water faucet. You should let the water drain until the water level is below the T&P valve.

Step 3: Release any excess pressure by raising the lever of the T&P valve, catching with a bucket if needed.

Step 4: Unscrew the copper or plastic drain pipe, if it is attached to the T&P valve.

Step 5: Using a pipe wrench, turn the valve counter-clockwise to loosen the valve, and then remove it slowly as there will be a temperature probe at the immersion end of the valve.

Step 6: Take out the new T&P valve and put Teflon tape on the male threads of the valve. Screw it into position by turning it clockwise, and tighten with a wrench. Align the outlet port on the new valve similar to the old valve, then attach the drain pipe to the valve.

Step 7: Turn on the water supply to the tank. If you have a gas water heater, turn the control back to the "on" position and turn off the water faucet you left open when only water and no air exits the faucet. If you have an electric heater, it is now safe to turn on the power.

2.8. CHANGING FURNACE FILTERS

Furnace filters prevent dirt, dust, and other airborne particles from clogging the HVAC system. More elaborate filters also enhance air quality in the home by trapping pollen, bacteria, and mold spores. The furnace filter is the first line of defense against airborne dust particles and allergens, and dirt that can clog internal components. Be sure your filters are kept clean as reduced airflow will adversely affect any heating or cooling system.

It is important that you check the furnace filter monthly and replace it as necessary. This will not only extend the life of your furnace but also ensure better heating and cooling during summer and winter seasons. Most experts recommend simple 1-inch (25 MM) fiberglass mesh throw-away type filters, replaced monthly, for maximum system airflow and ease of replacement by a homeowner. Most of the time the filter dirt adhesion is difficult to determine based upon visual condition – just replace it!

Here are the steps that you need to take to replace your furnace/air conditioning filter when it becomes dirty.

Step 1: Shut off the power switch located near the furnace/air handler. For filters located behind return air grills in rooms, simply move the thermostat setting to off. Replacing filters while the blower is operating can be frustrating as the filter will want to be sucked into the ductwork.

Step 2: Open the access panel or slot cover and remove the old filter.

Step 3: Now, put the new filter in place of the old one. Make sure the arrow of the filter is pointing in the right direction of airflow, which would be toward the furnace or air handler.

Step 4: Turn on the power to the unit or move the thermostat to the mode desired from off.

Tip: You can locate the furnace filter generally between the return air duct and blower cabinet/ air handler. You should write down the size and part number of the filter provided on the access panel, if that was done. Otherwise pull the filter and measure it. This will help you to buy the right furnace filter that is compatible with your HVAC system. Some systems have filters located behind return air grills located at ceilings or walls. Some homes have more than one filter.

2.9. HOW TO DIAGNOSE AND REPAIR ELECTRIC WATER HEATING ELEMENTS

Water heating elements are present in electric water heaters. The elements heat up water in the water heater tank. When electricity passes through the heating element, it meets resistance, which creates heat thus releasing it into the water. The amount of heat created will depend on the wattage rating of the heating element. The greater the wattage, the greater the heat produced by the heating element. Always replace water heater elements with the same wattage rating as the original element since the components and breakers are all part of the rating.

If your electric water heater does not heat, a faulty water heating element is the most likely culprit. Before replacing the heating element of your water heater, you should know the required wattage and voltage. You can determine the wattage and voltage on the water heater label and also on the end of the old water heating element itself, if still readable. In addition, you should determine whether your water heater uses flange, screw, or raised flange water heating elements. Take a photo of the existing element to bring with you to the hardware store when purchasing the replacement. Most of the time the lower element is the first to fail in dual element heaters as the lower unit works the most and can be affected by sediment in the tank.

Below you can find the steps needed to check and repair faulty water heating elements.

Things You Will Need:
- Multimeter
- Safety Gloves
- Phillips screwdriver

1. Diagnosing Water Heating Element

Step 1: Turn off the power to the water heater.

Step 2: Remove the access panels, insulation, and the plastic safety cover.

Step 3: You can now see two wires just above the red reset button near the thermostat. Try pushing the reset button. If it snaps that means it was tripped. Replace the plastic cover, insulation and access panel and turn on the power and see if this resolves the issue. If not, follow the steps below after performing steps 1 and 2 again.

Step 4: Use the multimeter set at 250 or higher VAC or higher at the two wire connections above the reset button to be sure power is off to the unit. Most water heaters are 240-Volt. Then set your multimeter to the lower end of Ohms or Ω. Remove any one of the wires from the water heating element itself. Now, place the meter probes on each screw of the element.

If the needle moves all the way across the face of the multimeter dial or above about 200, your heating element is the problem; you have to replace the heating element. Be sure you tested your multimeter when you set it to Ω by touching the probes together – the meter needle should not move or hardly move across the face of the dial (no resistance).

CAUTION!

You should make sure that power to the tank is turned off and wear safety gloves.

2. Repairing Water Heating Elements

Step 1: Turn off the power and water supply to the heater.

Step 2: Open the closest hot water faucet. This will allow air into the tank which will help it to drain.

Step 3: Remove the aerator from the kitchen faucet spout. This will prevent it from clogging when the water heater tank is refilled. Or use the tub spout, with the valve set to tub only on the diverter.

Step 4: Be sure you turned off the power and water supply to the heater.

Step 5: You should now attach a garden hose to the drain valve and run the hose outside to a point lower than the water heater or to a drain.

Step 6: Open the drain valve to drain water from the tank.

Step 7: After removing the access cover and insulation, remove wires from the heating element.

Step 8: Place water heater element wrench on the old element and turn it to the left.

Note: You may need to remove the four bolts if you have a flange water heating element.

Step 9: Unscrew the water heating element and pull it out from the opening. Sometimes the element is bent or covered with mineral buildup so you may have to tug rather forcefully.

Step 10: Place the new water heating element with gasket installed in the opening. Screw in the element by turning it clockwise until the rubber gasket touches the metal tank.

Step 11: Use the water heating element wrench to tighten the element.

Step 12: Install the wires on the new water-heating element.

Step 13: Turn off the drain valve and then remove the garden hose and turn off the closest faucet you opened to allow air into the tank.

Step 14: Turn on the water supply valve, and fill the tank. You should also turn on the kitchen tap or tub tap and let the water run until air in the line runs out. Replace the aerator.

Step 15: Open all the hot water taps in your house to remove trapped air inside the lines.

Step 16: Carefully check the new water heater element and make sure that it is not leaking.

Step 17: Put on the plastic safety covers, insulation, and access panels and turn on the power.

Things You Will Need:
- Garden Hose
- Screwdrivers, Phillips and Slot
- Water Heater Element Wrench (available in most hardware stores) or a socket large enough to fit the heater element hex

2.10. BLEEDING HOT WATER HEAT RADIATORS

You may need to bleed your hot water radiator from time to time to ensure that water flows properly throughout the system. Trapped air prevents warmed water from circulating through the radiator due to a condition called "air lock". Bleeding air is the solution for this problem. If you hear the sounds of water (like a waterfall) in the pipes when heat is operating, this usually means there is trapped air in the pipes or the radiator.

Here are some of the steps that you need to take to bleed the radiator:

Things You will Need:
- Small cup or a shallow dish
- Towel to catch spill
- Screw Driver – slot type
- Radiator key (square key for the air vent)

Step 1: First, you need to locate the air bleeder vents. On cast-iron radiators usually they are located near the top of the radiator and are most likely chromed metal. If you have baseboard radiators, open the end caps to determine if there are any manual vents. Sometimes with baseboard radiators there are no vents and in this case air removal is performed by purging at the boiler – best done by a professional.

Step 2: Now determine the method of opening the air vent. Some have a slot for a screwdriver, others have a square stub that requires a radiator key to operate. Some larger, usually brass or chrome vents, may be the float automatic type, and generally cannot be manually opened. If you have air in the system the automatic vents may require replacement, again, best left to a professional.

Step 3: Next locate the spout of the air vent, usually a small short tube protruding from the vent. Place a towel on the floor and hold a cup at this opening.

Step 4: Turn the opening screw slowly to the left until you hear air coming from the valve. Do not completely remove the bleeder screw.

Step 5: You may hear a sputtering or hissing sound from the bleeder, which indicates trapped air is being released from the hot water heating system.

Step 6: Note the status of the air exiting the bleeder. Once straight water is exiting the bleeder, turn off the valve by turning the screw to the right.

Step 7: Check to be sure the entire radiator is getting warm by turning up the thermostat. If the radiator is not completely warm, repeat the air bleeding process.

Step 8: You may need to perform this air bleeding task on several radiators. If your home has more than one level, it is best to start at the highest level.

CAUTION!

The water will squirt from the air bleeder valves. Once the air releases it can be very hot. Please use caution.

2.11. SIGNS OF IMPROPER COMBUSTION AND SAFETY ISSUES

Improper fuel combustion in HVAC systems such as boilers, furnaces, and in water heaters prevents proper heating, increases maintenance cost and can also lead to carbon monoxide poisoning inside the house. If there are any signs of improper fuel combustion in your home, you should immediately contact an HVAC repair company (or plumber for a water heater) to resolve these issues. Additionally, every home, in addition to smoke alarms, should be equipped with carbon monoxide alarms.

All fuel burning appliances should be safety checked and serviced annually, in particular, fuel oil appliances. Some of the ways you can detect improper combustion of your fuel burning appliance are described below:

Tip 1: If you find signs of corrosion or blackened areas near the heating system enclosure or the vent pipe, this may be an indication of improper combustion.

Tip 2: Flame marks and soot near the gas or oil burner is also an indication of improper combustion. Soot is nearly always an indication that carbon monoxide is being produced.

Tip 3: Any rumbling noise or rumbling from the heating appliance may be indicative of improper combustion.

Tip 4: Burn marks on the water heater, furnace, or boiler can also be indicative of improper combustion. This may be due to damage to the combustion chamber liner that presents a fire hazard in the home, or roll-out of the burner flame.

Tip 5: If the heating system frequently goes off on safety reset, this can be an indicator of improper combustion. At minimum it is an indicator that the unit needs servicing.

Tip 6: Smoke coming out of the heating equipment is also indicative of improper combustion and should be addressed immediately.

Tip 7: Excessive condensation at the inside of your windows could be a sign that the products of combustion, which include water vapor, are not being properly vented from your home. If you notice significant condensation on the inside of your windows, contact a repair technician immediately.

NOTES

CHAPTER 3: HOME ELECTRICAL APPLIANCE MAINTENANCE

3.1. IDENTIFICATION OF REFRIGERATOR NOISES

If you hear unusual noise emanating from the refrigerator, this may indicate the presence of some fault in the appliance, and the need for service. You need to determine the source of the noise to know whether the appliance requires repair. Once you identify the source of the refrigerator noise, you can determine the cause of the problem and potentially repair the issue yourself or contact an appliance repair person.

1. Noises from Outside the Refrigerator

Most of the noise from the refrigerator comes from outside the appliance. The condenser fan is the most probable culprit of noises from outside the refrigerator. Debris, dust, and lint can accumulate on the condenser fan causing it to make a buzzing or clicking noise. Cleaning the fan and condenser coil of debris, usually located under the refrigerator, will often correct this condition. Be sure to unplug the refrigerator prior to any cleaning activity.

A defective or failing compressor may also be the cause of noise from outside the refrigerator. If you hear rumbling or banging noises from the back of or beneath the refrigerator, and the refrigerator temperature is erratic, then it is most probably caused by a defective compressor. You should contact an appliance repair person to solve the problem.

2. Noises from Inside the Refrigerator

Inside noises are most often caused by the cooling fan. This fan circulates the air in the refrigerator to provide even cooling and prevent items on the bottom shelves from freezing. If you hear chirping, squealing, or groaning noises from inside the refrigerator, it is normally caused by a defective motor at the cooling fan or there is debris in the fan blades.

In order to make sure that the refrigerator noise is caused by a defective cooling fan, you must open the refrigerator door and press down the door switch. If upon holding the switch the noise inside the refrigerator increases, the fan motor is most probably defective or there is debris in the fan blades. This condition may cause improper cooling of the refrigerator and a qualified appliance repair technician should be contacted.

Other refrigerator noises occasionally occur which can be normal. An intermittent water dripping sound under the unit is most likely the defrost cycle. There is normally a small pan under the unit to catch the minor amount of water, which is evaporated by the fan under the unit. Some refrigerators will snap a few times upon closing the door- this is the seal compressing and it is normal.

Note: Most of the noise from the refrigerator comes from outside the appliance. The condenser fan is the most probable culprit of noises from outside the refrigerator.

3.2. DISHWASHER TROUBLESHOOTING GUIDE

Dishwashers are an essential appliance for nearly every homeowner. Like any other electrical appliance, your dishwasher will eventually fail, requiring replacement. However, you can prolong the life of your dishwasher by identifying and resolving certain problems well before they cause major damage to your appliance.

Here are some of the more common dishwasher problems that may lead to serious issues later on if action is not taken to resolve the issue.

1. Visible Cracks

Visible cracks inside or outside your dishwasher indicate a major problem with the dishwasher. Cracks may result in spilling of water on the floor, or cause water to get inside the enclosure causing corrosion and electrical safety issues. You should immediately call an appliance repair company if you find signs of cracks inside or outside your dishwasher.

2. Broken Handle/ Latch

A broken handle or latch will prevent you from closing the dishwasher completely. This may result in water spills and leaks that will seep through the dishwasher door. In some dishwashers, the latch is part of the appliance's safety system. The dishwasher may not function if the latch or handle is defective. It is prudent to get the latch repaired once it starts to show signs of becoming defective. Replacing the latch most often requires some dismantling of the door and is generally best handled by a qualified appliance repair technician.

3. Rust inside the Unit

Rust and other corrosion inside the dishwasher generally means the component is damaged or becoming damaged. If left untreated, it may develop further and cause serious damage to your dishwasher. It is best to contact an appliance repair technician when corrosion is noticed at the inside of the dishwasher, including the door.

4. Cold or Lukewarm Water

One indication that the dishwasher is not operating properly is cold or lukewarm water circulating inside the unit. The water inside the dishwashing unit should always be hot. If after a cleaning cycle you notice that the unit is cold or lukewarm to the touch, it may indicate some problem with the unit. Most modern dishwashers have control panel warnings if there is an issue with the water intake or the heating element.

5. Pooling of Water

Water that pools at the bottom of the unit is another indication of a faulty unit. It is normal for a small amount of water to be left inside the dishwasher near the bottom outlet grate. More than a few inches of water in diameter from the drain grate could indicate debris stuck in the pump, a faulty control panel, or the drain hose is kinked or clogged.

If the dishwasher is unused and left to dry out completely it may damage the pump and seals inside the dishwasher. If you are using a dishwasher that has dried out for the first time be sure to watch the unit for leakage.

6. Loose or Damaged Valves

The drain hose and water supply connections to the dishwashing unit may become loose or damaged with time. You should periodically check the hose and water inlet valve under the sink to ensure that there are no leaks. In case of any defect, you should call a qualified technician to resolve the issue.

7. Paint Peeling from Dishwater Racks

If you see visible signs of the plastic coating wearing off the bottom or top of the dishwasher racks, a quick repair will help prevent further damage. You can slip replacement tine tips over vertical tines, or use dishwasher rack touch-up paint to cover the peeling paint areas, after cleaning loose material. If left untreated, the racks may further rust causing small shards of rusty metal to enter the pump of the dishwasher, requiring costly repairs.

3.3. DISHWASHER MAINTENANCE TIPS

Dishwashers are generally a low maintenance electrical appliance. Most dishwasher problems can be avoided by proper maintenance and usage. With proper use, the appliance can last for decades requiring minimal repair and servicing.

Here are some essential maintenance tips to keep your dishwasher in good working condition for a long time.

1. Avoid Overloading the Dishwasher

Don't overload the dishwasher with too many dishes. You may have to rewash the dishes if you attempt to insert too many dishes inside the unit and overloading will block the water circulating spray wands. Additionally, there is a risk of damaging the dishwasher rack or rollers which may require costly repairs.

2. Regularly Clean the Interior

Regularly clean the inside of the dishwasher to remove bits of food particles or other debris that becomes stuck inside the unit. Use a rag dipped in household cleaner to wipe the space between the tub and the bottom of the dishwasher door. This location is more susceptible to debris buildup, as it remains untouched during the cleaning cycle.

You can use a sewing needle to clean the bits of food particles from the small holes of the spray arm. Avoid using toothpicks as it may break off and jam the hole of the spray arm.

3. Prevent Rust Stains and Organic Material Buildup

In order to prevent grime buildup inside the unit, you can use a deodorizer/cleaner made especially for dishwashers. In addition, you can use a rust-removing solution to clean off rust stains that may form inside the dishwasher.

4. Regularly Inspect and Clean the Drain Filter

The Dishwasher drain filter is located near the bottom of the unit or under the lower spray arm. Regular cleaning and inspection of the filter will ensure that it keeps debris from damaging the unit. Follow the instructions contained in the owner's manual to remove and clean the filter.

If you notice any damage to the filter, it should be replaced immediately. A dirty or damaged filter can allow debris to pass which could damage the motor seals and pump of the unit, requiring costly repairs.

5. Avoid Placing Plastic Storage Items inside the Unit

Never place plastic storage containers or other items that do not have the dishwasher-safe imprint inside the dishwasher. If the plastic comes in contact with the bot-

Note: Never place plastic storage containers or other items that do not have the dishwasher-safe imprint inside the dishwasher.

tom of the dishwasher, it can melt inside the unit and become stuck to the heating element. Removing plastic that becomes stuck to the heating element is not an easy task.   Clean plastic containers by hand or put them in the top rack to avoid contact with the heating element.

6. Never Use Dish Soap or Hand Washing Detergents

Dish Soap and hand washing detergents should never be used in a dishwasher. These are not formulated to be used in dishwashers. Moreover, they will produce a large amount of soap and suds inside the dishwashing unit which may spill onto the floor. You should use detergents which are formulated specifically for dishwashers.

Make sure you purchase brand name dishwashing detergent. Some discount detergents available on the market contain inferior cleansers which are not able to effectively clean the dishes. Buying brand name dishwashing detergent will ensure that your dishes get cleaned properly without causing any damage to the dishwasher.

7. Use Rinse Aids

If you have hard water or well water, you should definitely use a rinse-aid in your dishwasher. This will prevent streaking and spotting of the dishes due to buildup of sediment deposits on the surface from the water. Most modern dishwashers have separate liquid rinse-aid dispensers and control panel warnings when the liquid is needing to be refilled. Nearly all water supplies have some minerals, so rinse aids should be used in nearly all cases.

In older dishwashers that don't contain a liquid rinse agent reservoir, use solid rinse aids rather than liquid rinse aids. Solid rinse aids disperse much more consistently and evenly on the surface and are simpler to use with this style of dishwasher.

8. Add Vinegar if You Use a Water Softener

You can add 1/4 cup (240 ML) of white vinegar to the dishwasher before each load if you use a water softener. You may also consider reducing the amount of detergent you use in the dishwasher. Using vinegar during a quick cycle occasionally with no dishes loaded or detergent is also a great way to remove food particles and disinfect and deodorize the dishwasher.

3.4. MICROWAVE SAFETY & MAINTENANCE TIPS

Microwaves are another common household appliance found in most homes. These devices are fantastic for heating food and liquids quickly. Here we will provide tips and advice to ensure optimal function and longevity of your microwave.

1. Microwave Safety Tips and Advice

You may already know that putting certain materials inside the microwave is not safe. The materials may flare-up, melt or explode when they are heated inside the microwave. Some of the items that should not be heated inside the microwave include:

- Aluminum/Tin Foil
- Metal Objects
- Plastic not marked "microwave safe"
- Styrofoam

Some plastics can be dangerous and should never be placed inside the microwave. When plastic is heated it can release harmful chemicals into the food. If food stored in a plastic container is heated in the microwave, be sure the plastic is labeled microwave safe. This means the plastic has been tested by the manufacturer per US FDA standards and specifications for microwave use. You can use glass, ceramic, or microwave-safe type containers to heat food items in a microwave.

2. Microwave Maintenance Tips

Tip 1: You can periodically get your microwave checked for leaks, or purchase a microwave leak detector yourself to check. Microwave radiation can pose a health hazard in large doses if it leaks from the device, although this occurrence is rare. Regular checking of the microwave to detect leaks will ensure that you do not inadvertently expose yourself to electromagnetic radiation from the device. Microwave radiation does not make food radioactive –microwave radiation is non-ionizing and merely vibrates the water molecules inside food making them hot, which cooks food.

Tip 2: Keep your microwave clean to prevent accumulation of dirt, dust, and other debris inside the unit. If these particles are allowed to build-up, they may migrate inside the unit and damage internal sensitive circuitry of the unit. You can prevent dirt and debris formation by regularly cleaning the unit using a mild detergent and water. Pay special attention to the opening and edges of the microwave unit to avoid buildup of dirt and dust that may damage the door seal of the unit.

Tip 3: Look for signs of rust and corrosion inside the microwave unit. Rust erodes the coated metallic body of the microwave. It is advisable to contact an appliance repair technician to avoid causing further damage to the unit if you notice rust, or simply replace the unit. Newer and higher-end microwave models have stainless steel interiors which prevent rust formation in the unit.

Tip 4: Food items may sometimes get stuck inside the microwave. These items absorb some of the microwaves and may damage or cause burns to the microwave interior. It is important to regularly clean the interior of the microwave. For microwaves with stainless steel interiors, consider using a micro fiber cloth or a special stainless steel cleaner to remove food items stuck inside the microwave. Always follow the microwave manufacturer instructions on how to clean your microwave properly.

3.5. CLOTHES DRYER SAFETY & MAINTENANCE TIPS

You may already know that putting certain materials inside a clothes dryer is not safe. The materials may flare-up, melt or explode. Use caution when placing items other than the usual clothes in a dryer. Follow manufacturer instructions for unusual items such as shoes, bags, etc.
Clothes dryer lint screens should be cleaned prior to each use. Lint slows the exhaust of moisture and can increase drying time and energy use.

All clothes dryers should be vented to the exterior (not the attic or crawlspace), in particular fuel gas dryers to vent the products of combustion and the moisture from the drying process. Your clothes dryer vent should be metal. Older plastic vent connector pipes should be replaced with metal connectors. The "hard pipe" section of your clothes dryer vent should be cleaned by a professional regularly. Many home fires begin due to clogged clothes dryer vents. The longer your clothes dryer vent, in particular if it is vertical, the more often it should be cleaned. Consult a professional for proper clothes dryer vent cleaning intervals.

3.6. DEALING WITH TWO-PIN UNGROUNDED SYSTEMS IN OLDER HOMES

Homes constructed prior to 1965 in the United States may still be equipped with the original style two pin ungrounded outlets. Ungrounded receptacles are less safe than modern grounded system three-pin receptacles. If current leaks to metal, unintended current paths in appliances, or the house systems, the energized component or appliance can increase the risk of electrical shock and fire. A grounded electrical system and receptacles provides increased protection against electric shocks, fire, and also decreases the risk of damage to appliances in case of a ground fault – current leaking outside the intended path.

The ungrounded two-pin receptacles are outdated by modern standards, and do not provide a path for static electricity for modern computerized components, and most surge protectors will not work on two pin receptacles. Some homeowners use a two to three pin adaptor known as "cheater plug" as a quick alternative to installing grounded receptacles. However, this does not provide complete protection similar to properly installed grounded outlets. Another common layperson practice is replacing ungrounded two-pin receptacles with modern receptacles that have a third slot for the ground pin, but with no equipment grounding conductor connected to the new receptacle. This displays a false indicator of safety and does not provide adequate protection from the risk of electrical shocks and fire.

Upgrading the electrical system will not only bring it closer to modern safety standards but will also generally appreciate the value of an older home. Some of the other measures you can take to properly ground your receptacles include the following:

• Install three-pin receptacles and completely re-wire the electrical system so that a path to the source via equipment grounding conductor is provided to the receptacle.
• Install GFCIs (ground-fault circuit interrupters) in the home. These three-pin devices can be installed in place of two pin receptacles at the receptacle itself or upstream. GFCIs will provide additional protection against electric shocks even if you do not re-wire your home. If not grounded, GFCI devices and the protected receptacles are required to be labeled "no equipment ground". These labels normally come with the devices. Note that ungrounded three-pin GFCI receptacles do not provide a path for static electricity or surge protectors. Be sure to utilize devices designed for two-wire ungrounded systems.

CAUTION!

Homeowners should never attempt to modify electrical wiring of the home themselves if there is any question regarding proper procedures or parts. Electrical work should only be done by qualified and licensed electricians, and in some cases local regulation requires it. Any attempt to "ground" the receptacles to a grounding electrode rod, the neutral conductor, or metallic water line can be dangerous. Most any electrical modification will require that you obtain a municipal permit from your local building and safety department, and have an inspection by the municipal inspector.

3.7. WHAT DOES CIRCUIT CAPACITY MEAN?

Circuit capacity, also known as load capacity or circuit load, indicates the total amount of power that is safely available for electrical appliances in a home, through receptacles, lights and direct wired appliances. Your home may have many electrical circuits that have different capacities. Some appliances like your HVAC, microwave, kitchen cooking appliances and water pump motor may have their own dedicated circuits. In most modern homes a single circuit can provide power for six to fourteen outlets in one or many rooms, depending upon expected loads. For example, kitchens generally require higher capacity and multiple circuits due to the expectation of numerous appliances being used concurrently.

Total electrical capacity of your home depends upon the rating of the main service panel, service cable from the transformer, and the main breaker or fuses. This capacity is determined by the original installing electrician who performs a load calculation for the entire home and installs the appropriate equipment. Added electrical circuits can overload the system, so a licensed electrician should always be consulted for any modifications being considered to determine if a service equipment upgrade is needed.

Overloading the main panel or an individual circuit can lead to tripped breakers and may even cause a fire in the home. Fortunately, it is quite easy to determine circuit capacity of the individual circuits. Every circuit breaker or fuse has a label attached which indicates how much amperage the circuit is able to handle. Most circuits should not be connected to loads more than 80% of the over-current protection rating.

Upgrading the electrical system will not only bring it closer to modern safety standards but also generally appreciate the value of an old house. Some of the other measures you can take to properly ground your receptacles include the following:

- Install three-pin receptacles and completely re-wire the electrical system so that a path to the source via equipment grounding conductor is provided to the receptacle.
- Install GFCIs (ground-fault circuit interrupters) in the home. These three-pin devices can be installed in place of two pin receptacles at the receptacle itself or upstream. GFCIs will provide additional protection against electric shocks even if you do not re-wire your home. If not grounded, GFCI devices and the protected receptacles are required to be labeled "no equipment ground". These labels normally come with the devices. Note that ungrounded three-pin GFCI receptacles do not provide a path for static electricity or surge protectors. Be sure to utilize devices designed for two-wire ungrounded systems.

Note: In most modern homes a single circuit can provide power for six to fourteen outlets in one or many rooms, depending upon expected loads.

Next, you must determine the amperage rating of the devices connected to each circuit. The amperage of the device can be found using the following steps:

Step 1: Check the tags of each of the electrical appliances to be connected to the circuit and locate the wattage required. The tags are usually imprinted at the back of the appliances or a label on the cord. Some appliances even state the amperage on the tag.

Step 2: Determine the voltage of the electrical circuit. In the US, homes will have either 120v or 240v circuits, which will also be on the device label.

Step 3: Now divide wattage of each electrical appliance with the voltage of the circuit to determine the amperage. For example, if the wattage requirement of an appliance is 2,000 watts, then the required amperage will be 8.3 amps for 240v and 16.6 amps for 120v electrical circuits.

Step 4: Now add the amperage of all the electrical devices to be connected to a branch circuit. The total amperage load should be less than 80% of the total rated capacity of the circuit, usually printed on the breaker or fuse. If the electrical components add up to more than 80%, and there is a possibility they will be used concurrently, there is a high likelihood the breaker or fuse serving the circuit will trip. Consult an electrician if this is the case.

NOTES

_____

_____

_____

_____

_____

_____

_____

_____

_____

_____

_____

CHAPTER 4: ROOF REPAIR, REPLACEMENT, AND INSTALLATION

4.1. ATTIC/ROOF INSULATION ADVICE & TIPS

A well-insulated attic or roof rafter cavity can save up to 45% on heating and cooling bills. It can make a significant difference in increasing comfort and energy efficiency of your home.

It is important that the right type of insulation is installed to prevent warm and cold air from penetrating the conditioned space. This section contains some brief, but useful attic/roof insulation tips.

The amount of insulation that is recommended in your attic depends on where your home is located. Homes in colder climates have different insulation requirements than homes in hotter climates, although insulation can help keep heat out - as well as in - the house. The R-value (thermal resistance value) measures the extent of resistance to thermal conductivity provided by the insulation material. Higher values indicate greater resistance while lesser values denote lower insulation value, or resistance to thermal transfer. Most insulating materials have a standard R-Value rating per inch, and increasing the thickness of the material increases the R-Value, or resistance to heat transfer.

Many homeowners are installing radiant barriers in their attics. These are normally reflective foil sheets, sometimes with air-cell insulation sandwiched between the foil sheets, designed to reflect heat from the roof away from the house, and in winter help keep heat inside the house. Consider installing a radiant barrier if your attic configuration permits. Radiant barriers are also useful in unconditioned garages at the roof rafters to help keep the garage cooler in summer.

The table on this page shows recommended R-Values by the US Department of Energy (DOE) and the International Energy Conservation Code (IECC). The R-value for roofs and attics ranges from R30 to R60 depending upon the location of the home. R-value is determined first by the per-inch rating of the material used, then by the thickness of the material to be installed.

Apart from R-value, consider the type of insulation material. There are different types of insulation materials with different thermal or installation properties. For roof cavities, the most common types of insulation materials include standard fiberglass batts, foam boards, blown-in, reflective systems, or polyethylene bubble sheets. Most attics will have fiberglass batts or blown-in materials. Conditioned attics may have blown-in foam.

When considering adding insulation it is important to consult with an insulation specialist. The proper type of insulation must be installed to prevent compressing the existing insulation, with consideration given to the location of the vapor retarder, if one exists, to prevent condensation and damage to building components.

Generally, the vapor retarder should always be installed towards and touching the back of the warm (interior) wall material. If any bathroom or other exhaust fans in your house vent into the attic they should be piped to the exterior to prevent condensation.

All of Alaska in Zone 7 except for the following Boroughs in Zone 8: Bethel, Dellingham, Fairbanks N. Star, Nome, North Slope, Northwest Arctic, Southeast Faribanks, Wade Hampton, Yukon-Koyukuk

Zone 1 Includes: Hawaii, Guam, Puerto Rico, and the Virgin Islands

Zone	Heating System	Attic	Cathedral Ceiling	Wall		Floor
				Cavity	Insulation Sheathing	
1	All	R30 to R49	R22 to R15	R13 to R15	None	R13
2	Gas, oil, heat pump	R30 to R60	R22 to R38	R13 to R15	None	R13
	Electric furnace					R19-R25
3	Gas, oil, heat pump	R30 to R60	R22 to R38	R13 to R15	None	R25
	Electric furnace				R2.5 to R5	
4	Gas, oil, heat pump	R38 to R60	R30 to R38	R13 to R15	R2.5 to R6	R25 to R30
	Electric furnace				R5 to R6	
5	Gas, oil, heat pump	R38 to R60	R30 to R38	R13 to R15	R2.5 to R6	R25 to R30
	Electric furnace		R30 to R60	R13 to R21	R5 to R6	
6	All	R49 to R60	R30 to R60	R13 to R21	R5 to R6	R25 to R30
7	All	R49 to R60	R30 to R60	R13 to R21	R5 to R6	R25 to R30
8	All	R49 to R60	R30 to R60	R13 to R21	R5 to R6	R25 to R30

Source: NAIMA (North American Insulation Manufacturers Association)

4.2. ROOF SHINGLES INSTALLATION & REPLACEMENT GUIDE

Roof shingles are obviously an important component of the roofing system as they keep the home dry. It is important that roof shingles are installed correctly and maintained to avoid leaks during the rainy season. Roof shingles are available in many different varieties. Some of the common types of roof shingles in the U.S. and Canada include asphalt/fiberglass, stone, metal, concrete, wood shake, and plastic. Many areas require that the roof materials be fire-resistant or even fire-proof.

In the U.S., asphalt (sometimes called composition or fiberglass) shingles are the most common material used on homes. They are affordable, relatively easy to install, and can last for 20-50 years. Asphalt shingles can deteriorate quickly in areas that receive heavy rainfall or intense sun. Eventually asphalt shingles lose the protective granules and begin to curl or break off exposing the fasteners or material below allowing water to seep into the building.

Plastic shingles are not common and are often panels or sheets instead of individual shingles. Repairs of these materials are best left to professional installers. Metal, concrete and stone (usually slate) shingles (or tiles) are durable and resistant to both wind and fire. The roof covering types are relatively expensive to initially install, however, in the long run can be economical due to the increased expected useful life over other materials. Metal roof materials may be made of steel, aluminum, copper, or zinc alloy. Stone shingles (also known as slate) are considered one of the longest lasting shingle materials. Generally the flashings or other components will wear out prior to the slate.

Whatever the roof material you use, you should consider using high-quality flashing on the roof. Flashing refers to the application of metal or plastic strips to the house walls, penetrations, and chimneys and integrating it into the roofing material to create a weather-tight transition.

You can hire a professional to access and inspect your roof annually to determine whether the shingles need replacement or repair, or you can perform a visual inspection from the ground yourself if budget requires – recommended to be done in the spring and fall. Some of the things to look for when inspecting roof shingles include:

- Damaged, missing, loose or curled shingles
- Algae or fungus growing on shingles
- Rusting of flashing or parts that look loose
- Cracked mortar
- Dampness in the attic or other locations inside the house
- Parts of the roof found on the ground or in the gutters
- Plants growing from the roof surface and or gutters

Whenever you see signs of damage to the roof shingles or other components, repair is recommended. This will help ensure that water does not leak inside causing structural damage to the property and to provide maximum useful life to the roofing materials.

4.3. ROOF MAINTENANCE TIPS AND ADVICE

Roof maintenance is often ignored and leads to costly home repairs later on as most people wait until leaks occur. By the time a leak appears, other consequential damage has occurred beyond repairing the roof itself. The best way to minimize these expenses is to perform regular, routine maintenance.

Most of the time roof maintenance is best performed by a professional, as the use of special tools and access to the roof is required. Never use a ladder unless it is properly set on solid ground and you are comfortable climbing it.

Here are some maintenance tips to ensure that your shingles remain in good condition:

Tip 1: Keep branches trimmed away from the roof to prevent damage to the shingles. This also helps to prevent animals from getting on the roof and damaging the roof shingles or accessing the attic.

Tip 2: Prevent dirt, leaves, sticks, and other debris from accumulating on the roof. This helps prevents growth of algae on the roof, and allows fast drainage of water off of the roof materials. In addition, excess debris may clog the gutters preventing water drainage.

Tip 3: Remove thick layers of snow from the roof whenever it accumulates. Accumulation of snow on the roof could lead to roof collapse, severely damaging the house. You can use a snow rake to carefully pull heavy accumula-

tion of snow off the roof. When in doubt contact a professional.

Tip 4: Flashing is the main location for roof leaks. Check flashings around exhaust pipes, vents, and chimneys. If the flashing is punctured, bent, or the sealant has dried out or become loose, get it repaired before it allows water inside and leads to damage.

Tip 5: Consider installing zinc or lead control strips to prevent moss/algae growth on roof shingles. Most of the time the moss/algae does not damage the shingles, however, it does interrupt the flow of water off the roof.

Tip 6: Consider scheduling a yearly professional inspection of your roof.

Note: Most of the time roof maintenance is best performed by a professional, as the use of special tools and access to the roof is required. Never use a ladder unless it is properly set on solid ground and you are comfortable climbing it.

4.4. PROTECTION FROM SNOW & ICE DAMS

An ice dam can cause serious damage to both your roof and the inside of your home. It is important to stop the formation of snow and ice dams on the roof of the house. Snow and ice dams form from melting snow that refreezes at the edge of your roofline, creating a dam that stops water from flowing off the roof.

If this frozen snow dam is not removed water can back up underneath the roof shingles and get inside your home. Most modern homes have an ice-dam waterproof membrane installed under the first several rows of shingles to several feet past the inside wall of the house to help prevent any water intrusion into the home or exterior walls.

Ice dams should be removed whenever they form on the roof. However, keeping an eye on ice dams and removing them can be a dangerous chore as access to the roof is required. Here are some tips to help prevent the formation of ice dams.

1. Keep the Attic Vents Open and Ventilating

Ridge, soffit, and other attic or rafter cavity vents allow air to circulate under the roof sheathing. If the circulation of cold air under the roof is obstructed, this can result in formation of ice dams as the attic gets warm and the outer overhangs are cold, causing freezing. The vents should total at least one sq. ft. (.09 m2) of opening for about every 300 sq. ft. (28 m2) of attic floor, more in older homes. Cardboard baffles can be placed at the eaves in the attic near soffit vents to ensure that the air circulates under the roof without any obstruction by insulation.

2. Seal the Attic Hatch

If the attic access of the house is not sealed, it will create openings for heat and moisture to escape from the house into the attic and possibly result in the formation of ice dams. Cover the attic hatch using specific purpose designed weather-stripped insulated caps to help prevent formation of ice dams on the roof.

3. Make Sure Vents Do Not Exhaust Through the Soffit

Another way to help prevent the formation of ice dams is to make sure that the exhaust ducts attached to the bathroom fan, kitchen fan, and clothes dryer vents lead completely to the outside atmosphere through the walls or roofs and not at the soffits or inside at the soffit vents.

4. Ensure Proper Insulation

Attic or roof rafter cavity insulation helps prevent heat escaping from the conditioned areas of the house and warming the roof, causing snow melting which can re-freeze at the overhangs causing ice dams. Proper insulation of the roof rafter cavities and attic helps prevent the formation of ice dams on the roof, and saves energy.

4.5. PROTECTION OF ROOF FROM SNOW & STORM DAMAGE

If you live in an area where storms tend to occur frequently, you should take steps to ensure that your home is able to withstand these events. You should not wait until your roof starts to leak before preparing your house for the storm.

Here are some steps that you can take to help protect your roof from snow & storm damage.

1. Inspect your Roof
You should carefully inspect your roof for any damage. Take note of torn, curled, or missing shingles. The roof shingles must meet the local building requirements. They should be rated high for wind and impact resistance. Have any damaged areas repaired, and consult with a professional regarding the storm resistance of the materials where applicable.

Shingles and the underlying sheathing must be nailed down and fitted properly. Moreover, the connection between the exterior walls and roof system should be strong enough to prevent updrafts from lifting off the roof. Many older homes can be retrofitted with "hurricane clips" to achieve this strength in areas prone to hurricanes and tropical storms. Consult with a framing or general contractor for more information.

2. Check for Leaks or Water Damage in your Attic and at Ceiling Lights
You should inspect your attic and ceiling lights for signs of leaks and water damage. Although the roof of the house may seem to be undamaged from the outside, wind or rain may have caused damage to the areas under the roof. You should use a flashlight and inspect closely to check for evidence of water damage in your attic and at the ceiling lights.

3. Inspect Roof Gutters and Vents
Dents in roof gutters or vents may be an indication of roof damage. You should look for cracks, torn screens or weather stripping, and torn roofing that can allow wind and water in your house.

4. Consider Installing a Roof Deck
If your home is structurally capable, and the design works, you should consider installing a roof deck to prevent storm damage. The thickness of the roof deck should be 5/8", made of solid plywood with traffic coating. This will provide maximum resistance against high winds from damaging the roof. The roof deck and accessories will require proper fastening to the house structure to prevent it from being blown off in high winds.

5. Inspect Ceilings and Interior Walls for Leaks and Staining
Before winter weather sets in, check the interior walls and ceiling (including inside closets) for signs of leakage. If any are found have a professional inspect your roof and seal as many potential roof leaks

as possible. If the rooftop becomes covered with snow or ice, it will become difficult to locate and repair leaks.

6. Inspect Roof Decking and Fascia/Coping for Damage

Cold weather can have a significant effect on old mortar, metal, and other building materials. Materials may contract resulting in water leaks. Therefore, check joints on the roof and flashings for signs of deterioration, splits, and other damages.

7. Clear Dust and Debris from the Roof

Remove all loose debris from the roof, and be sure all accessories are properly fastened. Loose debris can be blown by high winds and cause damage to your house or your neighbors.

NOTES

_____

_____

_____

_____

_____

_____

_____

_____

_____

_____

CHAPTER 5: EXTERIOR ACCESSORY CARE & MAINTENANCE

5.1. MAINTENANCE OF WALKWAYS, PATIOS, AND DRIVEWAYS - TIPS TO AVOID SLIPS AND TRIPS

Maintenance of walkways, patios, and driveways is essential to avoid slips and falls. Although slips and falls are mostly caused due to slippery surfaces, they can also occur because of loose mats or rugs, cracks, offsets, and lack of traction on walking surfaces.

Here are some tips to avoid trips and falls on walkways, sidewalks, and driveways.

Tip 1: Place slip-resistant mats and runners on walkways if necessary to reduce the risk of falling due to loss of traction.

Tip 2: Keep the areas clean of dust, dirt, and debris. Dirt can cause organic growth which is slippery. You can remove oil stains and other contaminants from concrete to avoid slips and falls.

Tip 3: If there are offsets in the walking areas, such as from tree root damage, hire a concrete repair contractor to grind the concrete level to minimize the risk of trips and falls. Concrete leveling is sometimes a viable and inexpensive option.

Tip 4: Install a sloping ramp to reduce trip hazard at offsets. Remember that the ramp's elevation should not exceed an inch of rise per 12 inches of run. So, the slope of a 12 feet long ramp should not exceed one foot.

Tip 5: Ensure stair step riser height elevation differences do not exceed 3/8" or 9.5 MM.

Tip 6: Repair any cracks in concrete walkways and driveways, keeping in mind the size of a high-heeled shoe heel is rather small and can slip into a crack.

Tip 7: Provide secure handrails at all stairways for persons to grasp while traversing stairs.

5.2. KEEPING PESTS AWAY FROM THE LAWN

Lawn pests such as caterpillars, beetles, slugs, and termites are not just a mere nuisance- they may completely devastate and ruin your lawn if not kept at bay. The pests that attack home gardens can be categorized into two groups - gastropods (slugs and snails) and insects (worms, termites, beetles, moths). You can head over to your local garden store to stock up on chemical sprays and poison to use against the particular type of pests you desire to control.

Apart from using chemicals and poisons to get rid of pest infestation, you can also use a number of homemade remedies and non-toxic means of keeping pests away from the lawn.

Tip 1: Adding coffee grounds to your lawn deters slugs and snails. Apart from that, adding coffee grounds to the soil also increases acidity of the soil. This is great for acid loving plants such as blueberries, potatoes, azaleas, and rhododendrons which thrive in moderately acidic soil.

Tip 2: You can use chalk lines to deter ants from entering your lawn. The ants will not cross the chalk line since they are averse to

the calcite (calcium carbonate) in the chalk. You can also use cinnamon, baby powder, or slices of cucumbers to deter ants from entering into your lawn.

Tip 3: Certain plants such as Lemon Balm, Rosemary, Citronella grass, Marigolds, and Catnip have mosquito repelling properties. These plants suppress the surrounding scents that attract mosquitoes toward the lawn.

Tip 4: Placing crushed eggshells in the lawn is an effective way to ward off beetles and slugs. You should allow the eggshells to dry and afterwards grind them using a coffee grinder or food chopper. Finally, sprinkle the ground eggshells directly on the leaves. This will help deter beetles and other pests from making a meal of your plants.

Tip 5: Corn earworm is another garden nuisance that infests corn, bean, lettuce, and tomato plants. You can use vegetable oil to keep these pests off your plants. Just drip five drops of vegetable oil on the leaves of the plants. You can also add neem oil and spinosad to the vegetable oil to increase the effectiveness of the treatment.

Tip 6: Caterpillars can be a lawn nuisance. Putting Bacillus thuringiensis in the soil will help keep these pests away from your garden. Also you can plant umbelliferous flowers like parsley, dill and fennel to keep the caterpillars away from your garden. Parasitic wasps are attracted to these plants. These wasps lay their eggs inside the caterpillar's body thereby killing the host.

Tip 7: You can make an insect repelling spray by mixing four tablespoons of dish soap into 1 gallon (3.8 L) of water. In addition, black pepper mixed with pre-sifted flour also acts as an effective insect repellent and keeps them off your lawn.

Tip 8: Fritillaria, onion bulb, and garlic possess special odors that help keep four legged pests like rabbits, raccoons, and deer off your lawn. You can also use Cayenne, red peppers, and black peppers to achieve similar results.

5.3. CARING FOR YOUR LAWN

Your lawn needs some care to maintain vigor all season long. A lush green lawn helps create a beautiful and serene landscape around your home. Here are some tips to ensure that your garden remains healthy and green throughout the season.

Tip 1: The most important lawn maintenance task is regularly mowing your lawn. Regular mowing keeps the grass in good health. Trimming the lawn allows water to penetrate deeper into the soil. This helps the grass to endure dry spells and remain lush green throughout the summer season. Rotate the path you take while mowing the lawn for optimum effect.

Tip 2: You should choose a slow release, organic fertilizer and apply it to the outer edges and middle of your lawn. How much fertilizer to use depends on the type of plants and grass growing in the lawn. You could consider hiring a soil testing company to determine the pH level and quantity of nutrients in the soil. Your local garden center would be able to advise you regarding the quantity and type of fertilizer that you should use on your soil.

Tip 3: Low calcium-magnesium ratio in the soil results in outgrowth of lawn weeds. Presence of weeds in the lawn prevents plants and grass from absorbing nitrogen from the soil. Ideally, the calcium to magnesium ratio in the soil should be 7 to 1. If the soil test shows a low ratio, you can add high-calcium lime over your lawn to resolve the issue.

Tip 4: Remove sticks, leaves, and other debris from the lawn. They prevent sunlight from reaching the grass. Use a spring-tined rake to remove dead grass from your lawn.

Tip 5: You could use an aerator or pitchfork to spike the lawn. This breaks up compacted soil and ensures proper circulation of water and air to the roots of the grass. You should avoid aerating and removing dead grass during the summer season.

Tip 6: Use a water-filled roller to level your lawn. An uneven lawn not only looks unsightly but it may even result in damage to your mower. Be sure that the soil is wet before using the water-filled roller for maximum effectiveness.

Note: Regular mowing keeps the grass in good health. Trimming the lawn allows water to penetrate deeper in the soil. This helps the grass to endure dry spells and remain lush green throughout the summer season.

5.4. MAINTENANCE OF WOOD DECKS, FENCES, AND RETAINING WALLS

Wood decks, fences, and retaining walls add to the beauty of any home. These outdoor decors take a lot of abuse due to continued exposure to people, pets, rain, wind, sunlight, and snow. Without proper care and maintenance, they may deteriorate and become uninviting or even unsafe. Keep in mind any wood product has a finite life and will eventually require replacement.

Here are some tips to help ensure that your wood decks, fences and retaining walls remain in excellent condition all year long.

Tip 1: Use a stiff fiber bristle brush to scrub the surface of the deck, wall, and fence with a commercial cleaner solution. Consult the product manual to determine whether the surface needs to be dry or wet before applying the solution.

PVC or Composite decks and fences may require quick pressure-washing using a mild detergent. Make sure to wear hand gloves and safety goggles to protect your eyes and skin from harm. Do not set the pressure washer pressure too high and test the spray in an inconspicuous location first. Generally, a fan tip works best.

Tip 2: Remember to re-seal the deck, fence, or wall after it dries in around two to three days. You should drive in popped nails and repair split boards before applying sealer to the boards. Also, apply a waterproof UV blocking finish to the surface to prevent sun damage.

Tip 3: In order to remove dark stains on the deck and fence, you should clean it using soap and water. You can also use bleach-based products to get rid of stains.

Tip 4: You can remove dirt and debris between the boards using a knife or laminate scoring tool.

Tip 5: In order to clean stubborn stains from brick and other retaining walls, scrub the surface with a nylon brush using a solution of 2 tablespoons of liquid dish soap mixed in 2 gallons (7.5 L) of warm water. Rinse the retaining wall with a garden hose immediately after the cleaning process.

Tip 6: Pluck weeds off the retaining walls or use a weed killer.

NOTES

CHAPTER 6: CEILINGS, FLOORS & WALLS MAINTENANCE

6.1. MAINTENANCE OF GRANITE TILES

1. Cleaning Granite Tiles

Granite tiles add timeless aesthetic appeal to your house. However, cleaning these tiles requires proper care and precaution to avoid scratching or damaging the tiles. Here are some of the steps you can follow to clean your granite tiles and remove dirt, dust, and stains from the surface.

Things You Will Need:
- Scrub Brush
- Sponge
- Microfiber cloth
- A Bucket of Warm Water
- Dishwashing Liquid
- Safety gloves and goggles

Step 1: Pour a small quantity of dishwashing liquid into the bucket of warm water. Stir the water until soap bubbles form inside the bucket.

Step 2: Soak a sponge in the soapy water and thoroughly scrub the surface of the granite tile.

Step 3: Afterwards, rinse the sponge with hot water and again wipe the surface of the granite tile.

Step 4: Finally, use a microfiber cloth to dry the surface of the granite tile. (!)

2. Removing Stains from Granite Tiles

You should immediately remove any potential stain from the granite surface, otherwise, it could be nearly impossible to remove. Here are some of the steps you can take to clean stains from your granite surface.

Note: You can also use a specifically formulated granite cleaner instead of dishwashing soap solution to clean the granite tiles. Also, do not let alcohol or citrus product sit on the surface for long as it can dull the surface of the tile.

Things You Will Need:
- Hydrogen Peroxide
- Whiting Product such as Talcum Powder
- Water
- Small Bowl
- Plastic Wrap
- Tape
- Sponge
- Microfiber Cloth
- Safety Goggles and Gloves

Step 1: Mix hydrogen peroxide with talc in a bowl of water to form a thick paste.

Step 2: Apply the solution on the stained area only, cover with plastic wrap, and let it sit there for 24-48 hours.

Step 3: Afterwards, clean the area with a sponge and rinse with clear water, then use the microfiber cloth. If the stain remains, you can repeat the above process until the stain is completely removed, or try a commercial stone cleaner.

Note: Consider using coasters under all glasses to prevent stains on your granite kitchen tops. Also do not put any hot water, or hot cookware, on the granite surface as it may etch and dull the surface.

6.2. MAINTENANCE OF LAMINATE FLOORS

Laminate floors are relatively easy to care for and maintain. You should regularly clean your laminate floors to prevent them from getting warped or scratched. Here are a few general tips to maintain the good condition of your laminate floors.

Tip 1: Use acetone or nail polish remover to help get rid of tough spots like paint, oil, lipstick, ink, or tar from the laminate floor.

Tip 2: Never allow liquid to stand on the laminate flooring. Use a damp cloth to wipe any spill from the floor immediately.

Tip 3: Clean the laminate flooring regularly with a cleaning solution that is specifically designed for the laminate flooring and approved by the manufacturer.

Tip 4: Do not use the beater bar (for carpet) when vacuuming laminate floor. Instead, use a hard floor attachment to vacuum the floor.

Tip 5: Never use steel wool, or strong chlorinated or abrasive cleaners, to clean laminate flooring.

Tip 6: In order to remove chewing gum or candle wax from the laminate floor, you can use ice to harden the spot and then scrape it off the floor using a plastic scrapper. Afterwards, wipe the area clean using a damp cloth.

Tip 7: Never use a polishing machine or buffer on your laminate floor.

Tip 8: Use a floor protector or leg base roller on furniture placed on the laminate floor to prevent indentations and scratches.

Tip 9: Use appropriate color fill materials to hide minor dents or scratches on the laminate floor. Make sure that the color of the filler material matches that of the laminate floor and is compatible with the material.

Tip 10: Place high-quality floor mats at the entrance to prevent dirt, grit, sand and other substances that can otherwise get tracked in on the floor which can cause scratches.

6.3. MAINTENANCE OF HARDWOOD FLOORS

Hardwood floors greatly increase aesthetic appeal of a house. Apart from that, many homeowners prefer real hardwood floors for their sturdiness and durability. Here are some maintenance tips and advice to help keep your hardwood floors in excellent condition.

Tip 1: Wipe off any spills immediately using a damp towel. If water is left to stand on the hardwood floor for long, it will dull the finish and can damage the wood. Just make sure not to wet-mop the floor as it could discolor the hardwood, use a damp mop or hardwood floor dry buffer instead.

Tip 2: Applying too much wax on the hardwood floor can dull the surface. Apply a moderate amount of wax to clean the floor. Also, avoid using wax on a floor with urethane or other glossy finish, as this is the finish. Most modern wood floors do not require waxing.

Tip 3: Never use tile or vinyl floor cleaning products on your hardwood floors.

Tip 4: Place rugs near the doorway to keep dirt, grit and other debris off your hardwood floor which can cause scratching.

Tip 5: Do not walk on the hardwood floor wearing high heels, sport shoes, or cleats. It can cause dents and scratches on your hardwood surfaces.

Tip 6: Place a rug around the kitchen sink area to prevent water from damaging the hardwood floor.

Tip 7: Do not slide heavy furniture on the hardwood floor. You should pick up furniture when moving it around the house.

Tip 8: Place felt protectors under the legs of the furniture to prevent dents and scratches on the hardwood floor.

Tip 9: Avoid excessive sunlight exposure as it may cause fading and discoloration of the hardwood floor. Placing curtains and blinds on the windows helps prevent sun from reaching the hardwood floor. UV resistant coating of the windows is another way to prevent damage to the hardwood floor and other household items. Finally, you can place a rug mat over the hardwood area that is exposed to sunlight to prevent fading or discoloration.

Tip 10: Avoid using household dusting and cleaning products to clean hardwood flooring. Also, avoid using buffing machines or steam cleaners to clean the hardwood floor. Use tools and products specifically designed for wood floors.

6.4. REPAIRING A HOLE IN DRYWALL

Do you have a hole marring an otherwise perfect wall? Repairing a hole in drywall is fairly easy. With the right tools, you can patch the drywall within a matter of minutes. Repairing a small hole can usually be completed by simply filling the hole with drywall compound. For larger holes, use the following procedure.

Things You Will Need:
- Drywall Saw
- 6" (15cm) and 12" (30cm) taping knife
- Utility knife
- Sand paper
- Screwdriver, drywall screws
- Pencil
- Construction adhesive
- Drywall scrap, 1" x 2" (2.5cm x 5cm) or 1" x 3" wood scraps
- Drywall compound

Step 1: Purchase a scrap of drywall that is of the same thickness as your existing drywall.

Step 2: Cut out a square cornered patch that is large enough to cover the hole in the drywall.

Step 3: Place the patch over the hole and using a pencil mark the outline of the patch.

Step 4: Use a drywall saw and cut from the edge of the hole. You can cut in a straight line from each corner of the outline towards the center of the hole. Afterwards, snap back each drywall piece inside the outline and then cut it with a knife.

Step 5: Cut a piece of 1" x 2" or 1" x 3" wood strapping that is 6 inches longer than the hole. Squeeze a bead of adhesive along the face of the wood strapping and insert it inside the hole with the adhesive facing out.

Step 6: Carefully drill a hole through the surrounding drywall into the upper and lower portion of the wood strapping to secure in place.

Step 7: Now, press the drywall patch firmly over the adhesive and drive two screws through the patch into the strapping.

Step 8: Trowel a thick layer of joint compound over the seams, screw heads, and drywall patch using a 6" taping knife.

Step 9: After the compound has dried in a day or two, apply another layer of compound using a 12" taping knife. Smooth the compound 6"-7" (15cm) beyond the previous layer.

Step 10: When the final layer dries out, sand the area using fine silicone-carbide sandpaper. Afterwards, you can apply texture if needed and paint the area.

6.5. REPAIR OF RIPPLED CARPETING

Carpet ripples, buckles, and stretches occurs naturally with time as carpet wears. It occurs as the foam underneath the carpet breaks down and loses its elasticity. Heavily trafficked areas of the house are especially prone to rippling and buckling.

The following steps can be used to repair rippled carpeting in your home, or you can contact a carpet professional to do it for you.

Things You Will Need:
- Chisel & eye protection
- Hammer
- Tack Strips (possibly, not usually)
- Knee kicker or power stretcher for carpet
- Utility knife

Step 1: Remove all the furniture from the room that would prevent you from stretching and straightening the carpet and carefully pull the carpet from the tack strip at the wall in the direction of the pull. You may have to loosen from the sidewalls as well to allow for carpet movement.

Step 2: Place the knee kicker over the wall end of the area that has rippled or buckled. The knee kicker stretches the carpet as you hit it with your knee. For larger areas, you can use a power-stretcher to perform the same task.

Step 3: In case the rippling is extensive, you may have to re-place tack strips or padding of the carpet. Remove the old tack strips with a hammer and chisel and nail in the replacement about 1/2" off the wall. If the carpet is worn to the point it will tear, replace the carpet and pad.

Step 4: Use a knee kicker or power-stretcher to engage the carpet back over the tack strips.

Step 5: Finally, place the carpet down along the baseboards and fit it in place using a stair tool, cutting any excess with a utility knife.

NOTES

_____

_____

_____

_____

_____

_____

_____

_____

_____

_____

CHAPTER 7: BUILDING EXTERIOR MAINTENANCE

7.1. CAULKING AROUND OPENINGS

Caulking around openings helps prevent water intrusion and air leaks into/from the house. It is used to fill or close seams or crevices around the house. If the caulking of your house has cracked or turned brittle, you can take the following steps to remedy the situation.

Things You Will Need:
- Caulking Gun
- Razor Scraper
- Pad Scours
- Painters Tape
- Rag or Paper Towel
- Exterior grade silicone or polyurethane caulk
- Gloves

Step 1: Use a razor scraper to remove the old caulk. Remove traces of caulk residue with a nonabrasive scour pad. Afterwards, wipe the area clean using a soft rag that is dampened in mineral spirits and allow to dry.

Step 2: Place parallel strips of painters tape about 3/8" on either side of the joint. Now, point the nozzle of the caulking gun towards the joint and apply pressure to the trigger as you move the caulking gun along the length of the joint. Make sure that the beads are not too thin or have gaps in the seal strip.

Step 3: When you have applied the caulk to the entire length of the seam, you can use a damp rag or paper towel and press it along the length of the joint with your fingers to make it uniform, or use a caulking tool with the appropriate sealing edge for the joint configuration.

Step 4: Remove the painters tape taking care not to touch the new caulk. It will take around 24 hours for the caulk to dry.

7.2. EXTERIOR HOUSE TRIM AND PAINT MAINTENANCE

Most modern homes in the U.S. have low maintenance exterior finishes that do not require much care and maintenance, such as stucco, vinyl, and cement. However, homes that have painted trim and siding require proper care and maintenance to prevent deterioration of the underlying materials. The cost of re-painting a home is expensive and properly maintaining the painted finish can extend the life of the painted surface.

Tip 1: Regularly inspect the exterior of the house and ensure that mold or mildew is not growing on the surface. A household bleach solution can be used to remove mold growth on the exterior of the house. Just scrub the affected area with 3:1 ratio of water to bleach mixture using a stiff scrub brush and remove the mold and mildew growth from the surface.

Tip 2: You should remove dirt before it permanently embeds in the paint. If dust accumulates on the surface, it can discolor the paint and result in formation of mold and mildew. You can apply a low-pressure washer to remove dirt and dust from exterior paint. If dirt has already embedded in the paint, you can use a mild detergent and scrub brush to remove dirt from the surface. If the paint has failed in adhesion, the loose material will fall off as well.

Tip 3: Efflorescence, a white powdery mineral substance, sometimes forms on masonry walls from repeated wetting and drying. You can use a stiff wire brush to remove efflorescence from the wall. Afterwards apply a latex masonry primer and repaint the area, if it were painted.

Tip 4: In order to keep a fresh appearance of your exterior paintwork, you can regularly wash it using a commercially available house-wash per the instructions.

7.3. HOW TO KEEP VEGETATION OFF THE HOUSE

Plants and vegetation that wind their way up the exterior walls of the house may look beautiful but can cause damage to the wall by retaining moisture, adhering to the cladding, and allowing access for animals. The small branches of some climbing plants burrow under the paint and into the wall to get a foothold. This causes damage to the exterior of the house, and possibly inside the wall. In addition, if the climbing plants make it to the roof, they can dislodge the shingles allowing insects, vermin, and bats to make their home on the roof and allow water inside the house.

Here are some tips to keep vegetation off your house.

Tip 1: Trim unwanted vegetation as soon as it starts growing on the exterior surface of the wall. Climbing plants grow extremely quickly during the summer and quickly spread out all over the exterior surface of the house making it difficult to remove once established.

Tip 2: If removing the vines off the house would cause damage to the exterior surface, you can consider killing the vine by removing the roots first. This will make it somewhat easier for you to remove the vine and minimize damage to the wall.

Tip 3: Use herbicide if it is difficult to dig up the roots of the vines. Remember to wear goggles and gloves before spraying to avoid contact. Allow the plant to die for a month before attempting removal.

Tip 4: You can also remove climbing plants off the exterior surface of the wall by blocking access to sunlight to kill the plant. Cover the entire length of the surface where vines are growing with a heavy black plastic or tarp. Secure the material into the ground with rocks or bricks.

CHAPTER 8: DOOR AND WINDOW MAINTENANCE TIPS

8.1. MAINTENANCE AND CARE OF WINDOWS

Home windows require regular maintenance to prevent rot, corrosion, and other problems. Damaged windows can cause moisture problems, energy loss, and restrict use. Some windows, such as in bedrooms, are considered secondary egress in the event of an emergency.

Here are some useful tips and tricks for keeping your windows in optimal condition.

Tip 1: Follow the manufacturer's instructions before using any cleaning agent on windows.

Tip 2: Inspect, lubricate, and clean windows including mechanisms at least once a year. Annual maintenance could extend the life your windows.

Tip 3: Use a small paintbrush or vacuum cleaner to clean debris and dirt from the windowsill and track. Afterwards use a damp paper towel and wipe away residual dust.

Tip 4: Re-nail or tighten any loose channels attached to the side of windows. Be sure cladding joints are tight.

Tip 5: Use spray lubricant on window locks and mechanisms to keep the parts moving freely.

Tip 6: Avoid cleaning windows during direct sun. Sunlight can quickly dry window-cleaning solution leading to streaks on the window.

Tip 7: Be sure any moisture weep holes (small openings) at the exterior lower track are free of debris that might block water flow out of the window assembly.

8.2. FIXING STICKING WINDOWS

Wood windows can swell when exposed to moisture and rain. As a result, they become stuck and you can't open the windows or operation is difficult. You can follow these steps to help remedy the situation.

Things You Will Need:
- Soft Cloth
- Hair Dryer
- Candle or Beeswax

Step 1: Be sure the window is not painted shut, if so, use a knife to remove paint around the edge of the window sash. If not, try a hair dryer to dry out and loosen the swollen wood-framed window. Set the hair dryer to low heat and aim it at the sash located on the side of the window.

Step 2: Wiggle the window as you apply the hair dryer until it starts to budge.

Step 3: Use a soft cloth to remove dirt stuck on the window glides.

You can rub candle wax or beeswax, or use a dry lubricant, on the window tracks to help the window move more smoothly.

Step 4: In case the window will still not budge, then it is possible that the frame of the window has become warped or damaged. You should call a professional to repair or replace the window frame to remedy the situation.

8.3. FIXING STICKY DOORS

A door can sag or settle with time and may become "sticky" or won't budge at all. Fixing a sticky door can be quite easy. You generally don't need to replace the entire door to fix a sticky door.

Things You Will Need:
- Screwdriver
- 3" hinge screws
- Chisel

Step 1: Use a screwdriver to tighten the hinge screws attached to door and the jam, as these often become loose and cause door issues.

Step 2: In case the door hinges are still loose, consider replacing the screws on the jam with 3" (7.6cm) long hinge screws to reach the surrounding framing member.

Step 3: If the door still sticks, you may have to chisel the mortises of the hinge about 1/8" (3mm) deeper. First, remove the door off of the hinges. Then holding the chisel (3/4" [19mm] size) vertically in the mortise, make deep cuts across the width of the mortises. Afterwards, use a chisel and rock it back and forth to plow out the chips of wood.

Step 4: Attach the door back in place and tighten hinge screws. If this does not work you might consider hiring a handyperson to assist with the door maintenance. Sometimes the door itself will require trimming to fit the opening once the hinges are adjusted.

8.4. GARAGE VEHICLE DOOR MAINTENANCE TIPS

Garage vehicle doors are a large moving object and it is essential that they be well maintained and in good working condition. Regular maintenance of your garage doors not only extends the life of the garage door but also ensures reliable, quiet, and safe operation of the door. Many homeowners opt for regular inspection and maintenance of vehicle doors by a qualified professional due to their size and complexity.

Here are some of the important steps that you can take to keep your garage doors in good working condition.

Tip 1: Annually, lubricate opener chain or screw with a minimal amount of white lithium grease. This will extend the life of both the opener and the chain. Be sure to check the owner's manual as some door opener chains do not require lubrication.

Tip 2: Use a penetrating lubricant or oil to coat the overhead torsion springs mounted above the roller tracks. Coating torsion springs with cleaner or lubricant helps prevent corrosion of the springs.

Tip 3: Consider replacing the weather seal of the garage door bottom and sides if it has become worn or brittle. Remove old seal with a flat pry bar and place a new one in its place. Note there are differing connection methods for door seals so be sure to purchase the correct seal for your door.

Tip 4: Visually inspect nylon rollers of the garage door for cracks, chips, or missing rollers. On steel rollers, wear and tear of the bearings would indicate whether it would need replacement, usually they will be out of camber if failing. You can purchase replacement rollers from most hardware stores. Installing the replacement rollers is not extremely difficult. Just remove and reinstall the roller bracket to install the new rollers, one at a time.

Tip 5: You can test the balance of your door by ensuring that it holds halfway open without assistance. Disengage the electric opener first if one exists. If the door is not balanced, it will result in wear and tear of the garage door and opener. You can contact a garage door professional to balance the garage door if it does not stay in position when half open, which could indicate a defective spring or other issue.

Tip 6: You might consider installing a lift handle on both sides of the garage door if sectional type. When installed, you are less likely to place your fingers between sections to lift the garage door and avoid pinching.

Note: You should never remove the bottom roller bracket as many times the cable attached to it is under tension. Removing the bottom roller bracket can damage the garage door or cause injury.

8.5. REPLACING DOOR KNOBS

Replacing doorknobs is not as difficult as it may seem. You can relatively easily replace doorknobs with the right tools and equipment. Here are the steps that you need to take to replace a doorknob.

Things You Will Need:
- Power screwdriver
- Screwdriver
- Safety goggles
- Screws (these usually come with the new knob assembly)
- Door handle – the same brand will usually make the job a bit easier

Step 1: First, you have to remove the old doorknob. The doorknob is secured in place with screws located in the cover plates. If the screws are not located in the cover plate, then you have to push in a clip or key at a small slot located on the side of the handle. This will loosen the doorknob.

Step 2: After pulling off the doorknob, you have to remove the underlying plate. Use a flathead screwdriver in the slot and twist the escutcheon plate to pop it off and remove the screws holding the opposing parts of the doorknob assembly together and remove.

Step 3: Use a screwdriver or power screwdriver to remove the screws and take out the old latch. Then remove the old strike plate.

Step 4: Install a new doorknob and latch in place of the old one, in reverse order of the previous steps. It may be required to chisel slightly the openings to make room for the new knob assembly.

NOTES

_____

_____

_____

_____

_____

_____

_____

_____

_____

_____

CHAPTER 9: HOME SAFETY AND SECURITY

9.1. SMOKE AND CARBON MONOXIDE ALARM MAINTENANCE

Smoke and carbon monoxide alarms are essential home safety equipment that help minimize the risk of smoke and poison gas to humans by alerting their presence. Here are some tips to ensure that your alarms remain in good working condition.

Here are some of the important steps that you can take to keep your garage doors in good condition.

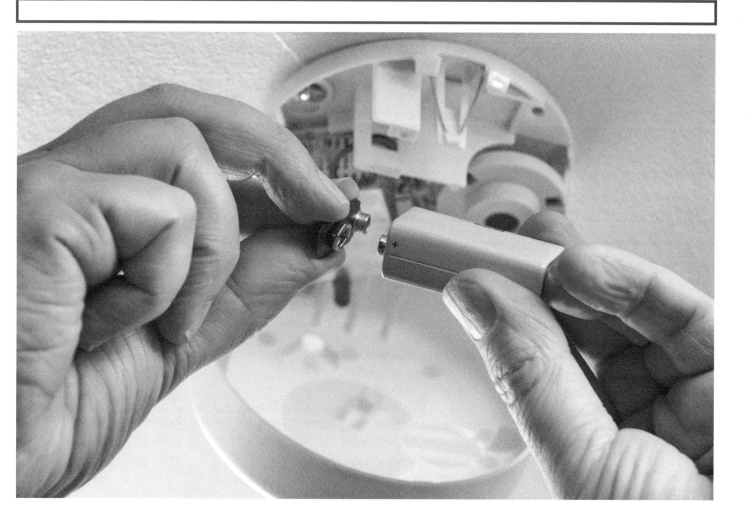

Tip 1: Check and test your alarms every month to ensure that they are in good working condition. Most hard-wired models have a green light to indicate the unit is powered and operational. Be sure your smoke alarm is a newer model that is a photoelectric sensor type, not the older ionization type. Photoelectric alarms are more sensitive to smoldering fires rather than flaming fires. Some alarms contain both technologies. Be sure all smoke and CO alarms have fresh batteries. Discard and replace any alarms more than 10 years old.

Tip 2: Clean the alarm with a vacuum cleaner every six months. This will remove dirt and dust that may hinder performance of the alarm.

Tip 3: If the alarm uses an alkaline battery, you should replace it every year. Lithium batteries work for a long time and should be replaced after about ten years. Many alarms now have a permanent battery and require complete replacement every 7 to 10 years.

Tip 4: Consider replacing your smoke alarms every ten years. The sensitivity of the smoke detector reduces during the lifespan of the smoke alarm. Some manufacturers place an expiration date on the smoke alarm. You should replace the smoke alarm at the end of the expiration period.

Tip 5: Be sure you have smoke and carbon monoxide detectors in all sensitive locations as determined by local building codes and the alarm manufacturer. Common locations are inside bedrooms and hallways outside bedroom, as well as the top of stairways at every level.

Note: Many alarms now have a permanent battery and require complete replacement every 7 to 10 years.

9.2. FIREPLACE MAINTENANCE

A fireplace can provide warmth to a room and can increase aesthetic appeal. Here are some tips to ensure that your fireplace remains in good working condition and keeps burning safely.

Tip 1: Hire a professional to sweep the chimney at least once a year if you use your fireplace often. Every 3-5 years if the unit is used occasionally will suffice.

Tip 2: Regularly inspect the cap located on the chimney. You can usually do this from the ground with binoculars. The cap keeps rain and animals out of the chimney. You should call a professional to replace the chimney cap if necessary.

Tip 3: Inspect the interior of the fireplace for build-up of soot and creosote. Soot and creosote accumulates inside the chimney due to the normal process of burning wood. They are flammable and therefore should be swept clean as soon as they build up inside the fireplace. Also check the firebox for any cracks or deteriorated components and have them repaired quickly. A chimney sweep can generally provide any fireplace services other than re-building the entire unit.

Tip 4: Consider using dry hardwoods like oak, ash, and birch in the fireplace. These hardwoods burn long and hot and tend to produce less soot and creosote.

Tip 5: If your chimney is older and made of brick consider installing a stainless steel liner in the fireplace chimney that has the ability to withstand high temperatures. A chimney sweep can assist with determining the proper type and material.

Tip 6: Consider installing heat resistant glass doors to help prevent heat loss from the house. You can also add a blower that will help direct heat into the room instead of most of it going up the chimney.

Tip 7: Adding the glass door also helps prevent hot embers from entering the room. Keep the glass door clean using fireplace glass cleaner and a paper towel.

Tip 8: Regularly clean the interior of the fireplace of ash with a shovel then with a vacuum. Wear gloves and a dust mask when cleaning the fireplace.

Tip 9: Don't store fuel close to the fireplace where it might ignite. Keep children away from solid fuel fireplaces and gas appliances.

9.3. MAINTENANCE OF HOME SECURITY SYSTEM

Many homeowner's insurance companies provide discounts if proof of an actively monitored security alarm is provided. Home security systems help deter intruders from trespassing in your home. Some alarms can also monitor home temperature and act as smoke and carbon monoxide alarms. Here are some maintenance tips for your home security system.

Tip 1: Perform tests of home alarm systems as suggested by the service supplier and always keep it turned on - it does no good if it is left off. Most alarms can be used when in the house by turning off the motion sensors and don't forget to fully arm the system when you leave.

Tip 2: Check that the security locks on doors and windows are secure by rattling the opening from the outside and see if you can open it when locked – repair if necessary.

Tip 3: Ensure that the batteries of the home security system are in good working condition. Most systems will alert you when the battery is low, or when it has lost AC power.

Tip 4: If you have a CCTV camera installed at your premises, you should ensure that it is in good working condition. Clean the camera lens to ensure that it provides a clear and uninterrupted feed. No plants or foliage should block the scope of the security camera.

Tip 5: Check that the sensors of the alarm are working properly. A number of home burglar systems come with motion sensitive monitors. You should ensure that they are in good working order. Many have a small red light that alerts you when the motion detector senses movement, indicating function.

NOTES

CHAPTER 10: HOME OWNER RESOURCES

10.1. EPA information regarding Asbestos and Mold

http://www2.epa.gov/asbestos

http://www.epa.gov/mold/

10.2. Expected Useful Life of Typical Building Components

www.huduser.org/portal/publications/rehabinspect.pdf

https://www.nahb.org/fileUpload_details.aspx?contentID=99359

10.3. Understanding Different Types of Insulation Materials

http://energy.gov/energysaver/articles/types-insulation

NOTES

NOTES

NOTES

_____

_____

_____

_____

_____

_____

_____

_____

_____

_____